Praise for
Never Settle for Normal

"*Never Settle for Normal* may be the key to help you doubt your doubting of God, because the god you are doubting might not be the real God. And if you lose reality while turning from the imaginary, you lose everything. You long for happiness and significance. Jonathan Parnell makes a compelling case that the whole history of the world exists to show you where this is found. This book is a journey from eternity to eternity. You may find what you are longing for not in a collection of ideas organized around themes but in a kind of earthy itinerary from creation to the end of the world. I hope so."

—JOHN PIPER, founder and teacher at desiringGod.org and
chancellor of Bethlehem College and Seminary, Minneapolis

"Jonathan Parnell shares astounding truth, making what it means to be a Christian understandable for any reader—from the wanderer to the veteran in the faith. *Never Settle for Normal* is a helpful primer and tool for anyone exploring Christianity."

—TRILLIA NEWBELL, author of *Enjoy, Fear and Faith,*
and *United*

"Jonathan Parnell has written an engaging book about our relentless quest for satisfaction that takes us down thousands of culs-de-sac and dead-end streets—until we follow Jesus. It's refreshing to read about God as a happy, loving Father in a book that doesn't minimize his wrath against sin. *Never Settle for Normal* shows sin for what it is and does, exalts Christ, and powerfully portrays his violent rescue of his people."

—RANDY ALCORN, author of *Heaven, Happiness, Truth,*
The Treasure Principle, and other books

"In moments of true awareness we look around at one another and this world and we *know*. Deep in our soul we know there is more than what we can see with our eyes. Proverbs tells us to get wisdom and insight; there is no quest as noble as this. The stakes are high and we need real help for the journey. Parnell's book is a trustworthy guide for all who are seeking God or any who are unsure where to begin."

—GLORIA FURMAN, author of *Glimpses of Grace*
and *Alive in Him*

"Most people I meet have a gap between the life they live currently and the life they believe they were born to live. The frustration that comes from wanting to live a life that matters, while seemingly never getting there, can be maddening. The way to bridge that gap is through *the* way, truth, and life—Jesus. Jonathan Parnell has written a captivating book to help show this reality. Read it, embrace it, and share it with someone you know who is searching for more."

—ALVIN L. REID, senior professor of Evangelism and
Student Ministry and Bailey Smith Chair of Evangelism
at Southeastern Baptist Theological Seminary

JONATHAN PARNELL

NEVER SETTLE FOR NORMAL

THE PROVEN PATH TO
SIGNIFICANCE AND HAPPINESS

MULTNOMAH

Never Settle for Normal

All Scripture quotations, unless otherwise indicated, are taken from the Holy Bible, English Standard Version. ESV® Permanent Text Edition® (2016). Copyright © 2001 by Crossway Bibles, a publishing ministry of Good News Publishers. Used by permission. All rights reserved. Scripture quotations marked (csb) are taken from The Christian Standard Bible. Copyright © 2017 by Holman Bible Publishers. Used by permission. Christian Standard Bible®, and CSB® are federally registered trademarks of Holman Bible Publishers, all rights reserved. Scripture quotations marked (msg) are taken from The Message. Copyright © by Eugene H. Peterson 1993, 1994, 1995, 1996, 2000, 2001, 2002. Used by permission of NavPress. All rights reserved. Represented by Tyndale House Publishers Inc. Scripture quotations marked (niv) are taken from the Holy Bible, New International Version®, NIV®. Copyright © 1973, 1978, 1984, 2011 by Biblica Inc.® Used by permission. All rights reserved worldwide. Scripture quotations marked (nrsv) are taken from the New Revised Standard Version Bible, copyright © 1989, Division of Christian Education of the National Council of the Churches of Christ in the United States of America. Used by permission. All rights reserved.

Italics in Scripture quotations reflect the author's added emphasis.

Trade Paperback ISBN 978-1-60142-906-3
eBook ISBN 978-1-60142-907-0

Copyright © 2017 by Jonathan Parnell

Cover design by Kristopher K. Orr

Published in the United States by Multnomah, an imprint of the Crown Publishing Group, a division of Penguin Random House LLC, New York.

Multnomah® and its mountain colophon are registered trademarks of Penguin Random House LLC.

The Cataloging-in-Publication Data is on file with the Library of Congress.

Printed in the United States of America
2017—First Edition

10 9 8 7 6 5 4 3 2 1

Special Sales
Most Multnomah books are available at special quantity discounts when purchased in bulk by corporations, organizations, and special-interest groups. Custom imprinting or excerpting can also be done to fit special needs. For information, please e-mail specialmarketscms@penguin randomhouse.com or call 1-800-603-7051.

To David Cooper

Contents

Though you have not seen him, you love him. Though you do not now see him, you believe in him and rejoice with joy that is inexpressible and filled with glory.

—1 Peter 1:8

The Stupid Normal

And I don't want a never ending life
I just want to be alive while I'm here.

—"Spirits," The Strumbellas

There is nothing necessarily wrong with normal. It all depends on how you're using the word.

A lot of times normal is good for you, like that garbage bag that needs to be taken out—the one with the little hole in the bottom that leaks a trail of some unidentified substance from the kitchen to the front door and demands an extra five minutes to retrace your steps on hands and knees with a paper towel.

Normal like that is an everyday sacrament meant to train humble hearts and level heads. That's why it's good for us to put on our socks one at a time, scrub the frying pan with a sponge, and stand in line for an hour just to buy a sheet of stamps so we can mail out our Christmas cards. This book is not about turning your nose up at menial things.

We need menial things.

Instead, this book is about not settling for the normal that has become our cultural mind-set. I'm talking about the kind of normal that pretends God doesn't exist, that casts a vision of life devoid of ultimate reality and then acts like we're better off that way.

I'm not talking about your nine-to-five job that feels boring. God bless your boring job—and I think most books that would tell you anything different are a sham. So I want to be clear from the start.

You're not going to find in these pages a message that runs with the whole "find your inner champion" glibness. You don't have an inner champion. You have an inner brokenness that desperately needs to be healed by Jesus. All of us, including me, are sinners who have bought into the lies around us, at least at some level. And if we're really honest, we've likely fallen for them hook, line, and sinker. That's because the lies are so many and so common that we don't recognize them as lies. They've become too normal. It's what I like to call "the stupid normal."

LIFE IS LIKE [A CUP OF HOT] CHOCOLATE

I first heard my daughter Hannah use this phrase when she was four. It was a cold Minnesota night as we were getting ready to leave our local YMCA. Hannah was standing beside her brother and sister as they waited patiently for our van to warm up in the parking lot, which is the sort of thing you do in Minnesota. The kids had been so compliant the whole evening that I promised them each a cup of hot chocolate when we got home. Hannah, however, was not impressed by my reward, so she tried to sweeten the deal.

"Can we get it at Ana's house?" she asked.

Ana was our girls' best friend who lived a couple of doors down. We had sipped hot chocolate with her and her family several times to wrap up afternoons of winter sledding, but on this particular night we just didn't have time.

"No," I replied smiling, "we're going to drink it at our house tonight."

And that's when she said it, with the unforgettable face of unfiltered disappointment. "But we just have the stupid normal!"

Now, my four-year-old was not a hot chocolate connoisseur. She had no extensive research on which to base her claim that the hot chocolate I made was somehow inferior to others'. In that moment she just knew that the hot chocolate she drank at Ana's was better than the stuff I made at home. Maybe it was the whole experience itself, maybe the company, maybe some extra marshmallows—I don't really know. But for whatever reason, my hot chocolate just wasn't the same. She knew there was something missing. She knew there could be something more. According to her assessment, our house just had the stupid normal.

And too often, that's what many of us would say about our lives.

If we were to sit back and consider our everyday routines compared to the depths of reality—the depths we've at least heard to be true—a lot of us might look as disappointed as my daughter. Even if we know the right things to say, we're rarely satisfied by how this knowledge contributes to the way we live. The grind of this life can get so monotonous. The labor never pays off the way we imagine it will. The vacations never deliver what we hope for. Even our most anticipated joys fizzle, leaving only fractured memories.

Is this it? Is this all there is? Something has to be missing. Surely there is something more.

We all wonder those things sometimes, even those of us who consider ourselves Christians.

We think about the bigness of this planet: all this life, all this action, all these sunrises. And then we take a look at the stack of trifles we've been buying into from this world: the ads that define the essence of joy, the pop lyrics that determine our value system, the magazine covers that set our standard for beauty. Not to mention the "calculated barrenness" being shoved down our throats.[1] It doesn't take much reflection to realize that all this air we've been breathing is a smog of lies. We've been running after something deep, but we're not even scraping the surface. The psalmist tells us it's the fool who says there is no God (see Psalm 14:1), and yet that's the anthem we've all learned to sing. It has become normal. That's why I call it "the stupid normal."

THIS WORLD IN WHICH WE LIVE

You shouldn't feel strange if you've felt disappointed about these things. Instead, you should feel strange if you have not.

This is the issue at the center of the human experience.

It's the issue our ancestors dealt with before us, and it's the issue especially worth dealing with today since we live in such a secular age—an age that has "progressed" beyond the need for genuine faith, or so it seems. We now live in this moment of history in which our everyday existence plays out in what one philosopher has called "the immanent frame."[2]

The immanent frame simply means that we live in a day and age when most people believe that what you see is what you get. It's the kind of thinking that says all the things *here* are the only things *real*.

And this perspective isn't entirely new.

Poet Walt Whitman, ahead of his time in the nineteenth century, wrote that there's never anything more "than there is now."[3] Heaven and hell might as well be here, Whitman would say, because *here is as far as we get.* There is nothing higher or deeper or truer than the things we can get our hands on.

Many people would claim to not think this way, but it's still how a lot of us live. Tim Keller, a longtime pastor in Manhattan, explained,

Individuals could profess to not be secular people, to have religious
faith. Yet, at the practical level, the existence of God may have
no noticeable impact on their life decisions and conduct. This is
because in a secular age even religious people tend to choose lovers
and spouses, careers and friendships, and financial options with
no higher goal than their own present-time personal happiness.[4]

In other words, it doesn't really matter where you see yourself on the
spectrum of religious devotion; the secular age has thinned out the faith
of too many. By and large, transcendence just doesn't have a seat at our
tables anymore. Instead, if we want the good life, if we want significance
and happiness, we're told we'd better find it in the stuff around us. "I
don't want a never ending life," as the Strumbellas put it. "I just want to
be alive while I'm here."[5]

Everything is *immanent*. That's the point. Everything is within
reach and earthly. *What really counts is just this world, and if there is a
God, well, he doesn't make much of a difference anyway.*

On a societal level, we have hacked off any true notion of the divine,
at least one that is pervasive enough to matter in the nitty-gritty details of
our lives. The idea of a distant God is fine and dandy, so long as he stays
out of our bedrooms. But as for that brand of transcendence where God
cares about what happens under the sheets, that is too divisive and con-
trolling. It's an intrusion upon the Self, which is whom we've hoisted up
to take the place of God.

This is called "exclusive humanism."[6]

We've decided it's better to make transcendence something *we* create
rather than concede that there is any reality outside ourselves. We have
tried to micromanage on the cosmic level and in the most backward,
tragic way. This is the way the world is now. This has become the new
normal, the stupid normal.

But as much as I disagree with this philosophy, I'm really not writing this book to bad-mouth the world. Enough people have done that and could do it for years to come, so I'm trying to not go there. At the same time, I'm also not writing this book to explain how we can change the world, at least not overtly in some concerted, high-adrenaline kind of way. You certainly can change the world, but it won't come by the clichés we see printed on T-shirts. My goal in this book is to help us live in this world. That's because this world, after all, *is the world in which we live.*

That's how G. K. Chesterton navigated the waters of pessimism and optimism about the world in his day. He simply called himself a "cosmic patriot."[7] He tried to be more loyal than critical. His example teaches us that whether we celebrate this world or gripe about it, it is inescapably *our* world; therefore, it deserves our commitment. We might despise it for what it's become and we might be weary of what it's made normal, but that doesn't mean we just keep complaining about it—and it certainly doesn't mean we settle for it.

But if we *don't* settle for it, what do we do? How do we lead our lives with significance and happiness when everything around us says there's nothing beyond the stuff we see?

BE SOMETHING AND BE HAPPY

Truth is, the reason so many of us think there must be more to this life is because, well, *there is more to this life.* Something *is* missing. We crave something we've tasted before. And the taste we miss, the deepest craving of the human heart, is rooted in the beginnings of time. It's a taste of glory. It's a longing for significance.

Ignacio knew all about it.

Ignacio is the main character in the hilarious comedy *Nacho Libre.* He plays a Mexican cook working for a Catholic orphanage while also moonlighting as a pro wrestler named Nacho (and nobody in the world could have played him better than Jack Black with a mustache). Midway through the movie, in Nacho's attempt to recruit a new tag-team partner, he asks a question that resonates with all of us: "Aren't you tired of getting dirt kicked in your face? Don't you want a little taste of the glory? See what it tastes like?"

Yeah, Nacho, we do. We all do.

Dirt in our face is actually a fitting metaphor for what the world offers us, and it doesn't come close to satisfying our souls. What the world gives doesn't add up with who we are. We have greatness in our bones. We've tasted glory before, and we want it back.

It's about more than glory though. Beneath and in and around our craving for significance is a craving to be happy. Blaise Pascal, the seventeenth-century theologian-philosopher-ninja, once put it like this: "All men are in search of happiness. There is no exception to this, whatever different methods are employed. They all aim for this goal."[8] And before Pascal, Saint Augustine, in the fourth century, shared the same conviction: "Every man, whatsoever his condition, desires to be happy. There is no man who does not desire this, and each one desires it with such earnestness that he prefers it to all other things; whoever, in fact, desires other things, desires them for this end alone."[9]

So the desire for glory, the ancients would say, is really about happiness. And I think that's right; the two are actually intertwined. We find happiness in our significance and significance in our happiness. The truest gladness requires meaning, and meaning is found in our capacity to be glad. The two go hand in hand. Our happiness bleached of our meaning feels arbitrary. Our meaning bleached of our happiness feels too abstract to understand.

Jonathan Haidt, author of *The Happiness Hypothesis,* gets at this same point. Haidt is a leader in a new positive-psychology movement that attempts to help people find happiness and meaning.[10] *The* question of all questions—he calls it the "Holy Question"—is "What is the meaning of life?" Everyone should want to find an answer, he argues, and the hope, he says, is that all of us will discover something enlightening about who we are and what we're doing in this world.[11]

Each of us, in one way or another, is searching for the secret sauce, the silver bullet, whatever that thing is that will quench our thirst for significance and pleasure. We all want a "good, *happy,* fulfilling, and *meaningful* life."[12]

But we're not going to find that in the mainstream culture.

There is, however, another path, one different from the one most commonly traveled in this secular age. And that path is found in the Christian story.

BIG BRUSH, BRIGHT COLORS

Dorothy Sayers once wrote, "The Christian faith is the most exciting drama that ever staggered the imagination of man—and the dogma is the drama."[13] Sayers understood that the essential pieces of Christian dogma, or doctrine, are inherently dramatic.[14] She saw that the basic tenets of Christian theology are actually scenes within a greater narrative, and this greater narrative isn't exactly a bedtime story. It's a narrative full of brokenness and beauty, despair and hope, darkness and light. It's a story we all live in, which means, one way or the other, we're all journeying somewhere. *We're living in this story, and we're going somewhere.* And our lives at some point, in whatever age we might exist, will come to a clearing. There is a path we should know about. It's not an easy path, but many have walked it before us, and it's the only path that has the answers to our souls' deepest longings.

So that's what this book is about.

Over the next ten chapters, I will introduce to you the central parts of the Christian story, but not in the form of bland bullet points. I want you to encounter each doctrine as a milestone along a journey, leading us to the significance and happiness for which we were made.

Though originally shared in a language we don't speak and told from the perspective of a culture and age different from our own, the truths you're about to encounter speak to our greatest need. They form a path that resonates with our souls. These truths show us what's missing, where to find it, and how we might experience something truer and better in this life—something much truer and better than the stupid normal.

2

When You Think About God

> To go wrong in one's doctrine of
> God is to go wrong everywhere.
>
> —Kevin Vanhoozer

God   me

Something just happened when you saw those two words. The official term for it is *associative activation.*

You came across two words and immediately began to associate one with the other. You didn't have to think about it; you just did it, and you do it all the time. It's how we make sense of the world around us. We see words, images, and objects, and in our minds we attempt to form coherent relationships among them.

Let me give you an example.

Bread . . . peanut butter . . . jelly—okay, that's food. Actually, it's a sandwich. No, it's lunch for the kids. My wife is making lunch for the kids because it's noon and the kids are hungry. It looks like the jelly jar is over half empty. We should get jelly the next time we go to the grocery store because you can't have PB&Js without jelly. I'd better write that down so I don't forget.

And then we move on to the next thing and repeat a similar process. It's something we do automatically.

Psychologist Daniel Kahneman explained that during this process of associative activation, one idea triggers many other ideas, creating a "spreading cascade of activity in your brain."[1]

So think back to the beginning of this chapter. You saw two words sitting side by side:

God   me

Once you saw these words, you probably started wondering:

- *Why are these words here?*
- *Is a verb missing?*
- *What does this mean?*

Chances are you eventually arrived at a question like this: *What does God have to do with me?*

You were presented with a blank space that you were compelled to fill. God *does* have something to do with you, and when you filled in that something, whatever it might have been, you constructed a sentence. Or really, you told a mini-story. We all have a story about how we think we are connected to God, and whatever that story is, it starts with what we think about God.

WHAT ABOUT HIM?

Years ago there was an author who said that whatever it is you think when you think about God, *that* is the most important thing about you.[2] We all have some concept about him deep in our gut, something we think without having to think about it. Whether or not you believe it's the most important thing about you, we can all agree that it in some way affects the way you live. It would be silly to think this isn't the case, especially in light of the world at large. For most people in most cultures, throughout much of human history, the greatest force shaping their lives is their view of Ultimate Reality. Why would we Westerners of the twenty-first century think we're an exception?

We're not.

The conversation might look different. The context certainly isn't the same. But it's true: what we think about God is still a game changer for us. Whether we believe God is real or we don't, that still has an impact on us. And therefore, if we're playing fair, we should give him some thought.

So then, what do you think when you think about God? What is the first image that comes to your mind?

Maybe you think nothing. Or you want to think nothing, but then it gets weird because you can't just think of nothing, and the nothing you try to think about becomes this incoherent montage of images being swallowed by an amorphous black hole.

Or maybe you think *Creator*. You think of everything in this world, the trees and the slugs and the insanity of how marsupials raise their offspring, and you see God as the One behind it all. He is the great Source, the unmoved Mover.

Or maybe you think about all the benevolence in the world. You've seen love and goodness in the things around you. You're spiritual enough to recognize that there's some deep stuff happening out there, but you fall back on that blind-men-touching-an-elephant analogy: some have their hands on its trunk, others on its legs, and it's just not right to prefer one interpretation over another.

Or perhaps you think God is a tyrant. Maybe you imagine him as a grouchy drill sergeant up in the sky.

Or possibly you see God as a figment of defective minds, the opium of the masses.

Whatever you think about God affects how you live. And I'm refer-ring to what you *automatically* think about God, not what you know you *should* think. The contours of a healthy theology do little good if we can get to them only by scrambling over how we really feel. It's our instinctive notion of God that pulls from something deeper than learned truths. That first thought is our own big brushstroke. It's how we imagine God from the core of our being, without assembling the data and doing the math. That first thought is the one that influences us the most.

And if we acknowledge that our view of God bears some importance in our lives, shouldn't we at least check that view with what the Bible has to say about him? The Bible is, after all, God's autobiography, spanning sixty-six collected works of various sizes, composed by multiple human authors, written over centuries in three original languages, copied and preserved through wars, disease, and climate change to be made available today, for you, in modern English.

I think it deserves our attention.

The Bible is just too peculiar and its influence too pervasive to not give it a hearing. Because this is the case (notwithstanding that I believe it is from God), the Bible serves as the foundation for how I'm going to talk about God in this book. The Bible is where I get my information.

There is a lot of freight behind why I'm basing our discussion of God on the Bible, but my simplest reason is that we ourselves are incapable of uncovering a reliable picture of who God is. But even if we did, we should know better than to believe that a concept of a deity we come up with ourselves is one we can trust.

The Voilà of Preference

Even though we can't trust a god we invent ourselves, many of us are still trying to contrive a god that's suitable to us. We want to piece him together. We include all the things we would like to see, discard those traits that make us uncomfortable, and then voilà: we have a higher being we can get along with.

The ironic result is that our societal conscience, which is so reluctant to declare anything certain or absolute, never admits that our self-constructed idea of God could be wrong. In fact, in an even stranger twist, it seems the only picture of God that people doubt is the one that comes from the Bible, which is the only picture we get from outside ourselves. Do you see the irony in this?

There are probably several reasons for this, but perhaps the main reason we so easily doubt a picture of God *from outside ourselves* is because we know that only such a God can have real authority over our lives.

We know deep down that if we're the ones who invent "God," then we're the ones calling the shots. Basically, we know that the god of our making is a toothless teddy bear in the sky who minds his own business. It may even be that many who talk about the "intellectual incongruity of theism" use it as a smoke screen. Maybe it's not so much that they can't intellectually grasp God's existence but more that they just want to do what they want to do. Humans are not just thinkers, you know. We feel. We desire. And we don't like authority telling us how to live our lives. Deep down, we're all like little kids.

I WANT TO BE AN ORPHAN

My own kids continue to teach me this. Awhile back I heard one of our children (who will remain unnamed to protect the guilty) arguing with her siblings over toys. One kid wanted the toy that the other kid had. The complaint grew until it reached parental appeal. So I stepped in and suggested that we all take turns. Now, if you're a parent, you know that the whole concept of sharing baffles the heck out of kids. The thought of giving someone else something that *I* want, in the moment when *I* want it, can cause outrage in the younger among us. Something like that happened here.

My kid prosecutor, annoyed by my counsel to share, mumbled under her breath, "I wish I didn't have a mommy and daddy."

"What?" I asked. I must have misheard.

My kid doubled down: "I wish I was an orphan!"

At that point I realized that my beloved child had not thought this through. She hadn't bothered to step back and consider all the implications of not having parents. All she cared about in that moment was that her dad was standing in the way of something she wanted. Kids are feelers like that. In that situation, my child knew she wanted the toy for herself, and therefore she didn't want me to exist. She wanted to be an orphan.

"I want to be an orphan"—that sounds too eerily like the anthem of exclusive humanism. It sounds like the music of an age that has tried to get rid of God. Isn't that what we're saying when we try to make it in this world without him? Could it be that we're so stuck on what we think we want that we're blind to what we're actually bargaining for?

I think this is a crucial question.

Is our skepticism, which dresses up so nicely, really as decent as it appears? Shouldn't our cynicism at least cast its shadow with equity? Shouldn't we stop to share the doubt—not just doubting God but also doubting our actual doubting of God?

This is a really crucial question.

I think it would help us to back up a few steps and take a fresh look at what the Bible says about God. Whatever your background is, churched or unchurched, newly churched, dechurched, or agnostic, it doesn't matter. It's only fair and wise to hear what God says about himself.

The Happy Father Who Loves

> Do we want God in our own image or do we
> want the God who is beyond us and over us,
> who we trust will do for us what only God can
> do in the way that only God can do it—no
> strings attached . . . no reservations . . . no
> caveats . . . the whole hog?
>
> —Eugene Peterson

The Bible has a lot to say about how we should picture God. That is really the whole point. God is the Creator (see Psalm 90:2). He is the sovereign, covenant-keeping Shepherd (see Ezekiel 34:15). He is the King, our Redeemer, and the Husband of his people (see Isaiah 6:5; 41:14; Hosea 2:16).

When we take all the pictures together, we actually begin to see two complementary categories emerge for how we think of him. First, there is who God is *because of what he does*. It's mainly functional. This is the category of God in relation to other things. And second, there is who God is *apart from anything else*. This is God in his essence.

The images of God as Creator, Shepherd, and Redeemer are wonderfully true pictures of him that the Bible gives us. Categorically, though, they are pictures of God in relation to other things. To be a Creator requires things that were created. To be a Shepherd requires sheep (sheep is a repeated metaphor for God's people). In both cases, there has to be something outside of God to help form the picture of God.

But who is God apart from other things? What is God's essence? When we start looking at God from this perspective, three basic pictures come into view.

GOD IS FATHER

We begin to drill down to the foundation of God's essence when we understand that God is Father.[1] The Bible is straightforward here, and we can see this picture emerge first in the Old Testament. Psalms portrays the fatherhood of God in passages such as 89:26, when God's anointed king prayed, "You are my Father, my God, and the Rock of my salvation." There are also poetic uses, including 103:13: "As a father shows compassion to his children, so the LORD shows compassion to those who fear him." The prophet Isaiah prayed, "You, O LORD, are our Father, our Redeemer from of old is your name" (63:16). He wrote later, "But now, O LORD, you are our Father; we are the clay, and you are our potter; we are all the work of your hand" (64:8).

These are beautiful passages. I love the poetic literature of the Old Testament. But I think the most amazing way God is seen as a Father is in the New Testament, in relation to Jesus. We see it first in the baptism of Jesus, as told by the gospel writer Matthew. Before the word *Father* is mentioned explicitly in reference to God, we hear a father's voice call out from heaven. God said, "This is my beloved Son, with whom I am well pleased" (3:17). Later, Jesus told us, in words more profound than we often grasp, "Let your light shine before others, so that they may see your good works and give glory to *your Father* who is in heaven" (5:16).

Jesus called God "our Father." God is both his Father and ours. That's also how Jesus taught his disciples to pray: "Our Father in heaven" (6:9).

But wait a second. If we call God "Father," doesn't that also require something outside of himself? Just as God being a Creator means he must have creatures, doesn't God being a Father mean he must have children?

Well, yes, but here's the thing: for God to be a Father, he doesn't depend on anything outside of himself. He is a Father in his essence. In fact, in light of what the Bible shows us, we understand that God is an everlasting Father who has eternally loved his Son in the unceasing fellowship of the Spirit (see John 17:24; Romans 5:5; 1 John 1:3).

The reason that God *as Father* is God *in his essence* is because the Son that God has eternally loved is actually *in himself,* not outside of himself. This is because God is essentially triune, which is the ancient word in Christian theology that attempts to capture the mystery of God as three in one. The Athanasian Creed, written in the early sixth century, puts it this way: "We worship one God in trinity and the trinity in unity, neither blending their persons nor dividing their essence. For the person of the Father is a distinct person, the person of the Son is another, and that of the Holy Spirit still another. But the divinity of the Father, Son, and Holy Spirit is one, their glory equal, their majesty coeternal."[2] God is a Father *within himself* because within himself, *essentially,* he is Father, Son, and Spirit.

Okay, look, this is deep water. I get it. You grabbed a small paperback book and perhaps kicked back for some light reading. Hang in there, though. We're headed somewhere. This topic of the Trinity is wonderful and glorious, and it leads to far-reaching implications connected to every facet of reality. But the point I want to highlight here is that this picture of God helps us form our first take on who he is. I'm talking about the thought or picture that first pops into our heads when we think about God.

If we let the Bible form how we think about him—if we let *God is Father* become that first thought—then we will see him as a God who fundamentally cares about relationships. We will see him as a personal being, not a distant deity out of touch with our lives. He is a God who has never done anything arbitrary. He has never done anything out of an isolated, self-centered will. Instead, he is a God who is involved. He is a God who, in his essence, is aware. He is a God who takes an interest in what comes into your mind when you first think of him.

Relationship is at the heart of who he is, the God triune—the Father who loves his Son in the fellowship of the Spirit.

GOD IS HAPPY

It is one thing to see that God is essentially relational, but what *kind* of Father is he?

He is a happy Father.

We can see this in a fascinating phrase from the apostle Paul's first letter to his friend Timothy. Paul had been exhorting Timothy on sound doctrine "in accordance with the gospel of the glory of *the blessed God* with which I have been entrusted" (1:11).

The Greek word translated "blessed" literally means "happy." It's the same word Jesus used in his famous Sermon on the Mount found in Matthew 5: "*Blessed* are the poor in spirit, for theirs is the kingdom of heaven. *Blessed* are those who mourn, for they shall be comforted. *Blessed* are the meek, for they shall inherit the earth" (verses 3–5), and so on.

In this sermon Jesus described people who are blessed (happy!), and then he gave the rationale: *because* theirs is the kingdom of heaven, *because* they shall be comforted, *because* they shall inherit the earth. The blessed one is the happy one. That's what Jesus was saying.

So when the apostle Paul said in his letter to Timothy that God is the blessed God, he was saying that God is the happy God. The gospel is the gospel of the glory of the happy God. And the reason Paul called God happy is because God *is* happy.

Now, you might not think about happiness when you think about God.

Many of us, I'd guess, are more influenced by *The Wizard of Oz* than the Bible when it comes to our initial thought about who God is.

You may remember the scene in the classic 1939 movie when Dorothy and her friends go to see the wizard that second time. Dorothy, the sweet Kansas girl, along with the Tin Man, the Lion, and the Scarecrow, had all been searching for something—for home, for a heart, for courage, for a brain—and by the end of the movie they've done what they were supposed to do in order to get what they wanted. It was Oz's turn to keep his end of the deal.

"Please, sir," Dorothy says, "we've done what you told us. We've brought you the broomstick of the Wicked Witch of the West."

But it's not that easy.

Flames blaze and smoke bellows. Oz, "the great and powerful," with a frowning face, replies in a cranky voice, "Not so fast! Not so fast!" Then he tries to put them off, saying, "Go away and come back tomorrow!"

Oz turns out to be quite the humbug.

But then, behind the curtain, thanks to Toto the dog, they discover that the wizard is actually a scatterbrained old man pretending to be something he's not. All bark and no bite. If Oz were real he'd be ornery, but he's not real, and his personality is so disappointing that it's a relief to find out he's a fake.

That's the Wizard of Oz. But that's not how it is with God. The Bible tells us that God is happy. He doesn't hide behind a curtain, and he doesn't speak with a formidable frown. The baptism of Jesus once again helps us with the picture. Listen again to the voice that called out from heaven: "This is my beloved Son, with whom I am well pleased" (Matthew 3:17).

God the Father wants us to know that he is delighted in God the Son.

Then in a later scene, in another earth-shaking moment, when Jesus is transfigured in front of a few of his disciples, God the Father said it again: "This is my beloved Son, with whom I am well pleased" (17:5).

Put simply, the verse says, "This is my Son, whom I love and whom I enjoy." Eugene Peterson paraphrased it, "This is my Son, marked by my love, focus of my delight" (MSG).

And then again, in the gospel according to Luke, we see another snapshot of God's gladness. Jesus told his disciples that "there is joy in the presence of the angels of God over one sinner who repents" (15:10, NRSV). This means that every time a person turns from his or her sins and believes the good news of Jesus, God himself rejoices. The angels are in the company of God, and if joy is in their presence, it's because God the Father is glad.

Earlier in Luke's gospel, we hear Jesus's message to anxiety-ridden souls as he laid out a foundation for how to live a worry-free life: "Fear not, little flock, for it is your Father's good pleasure to give you the kingdom" (12:32). In other words, Jesus said, "Don't be afraid, because your Father delights to give you the kingdom." The Father delights—takes pleasure in—giving us the most important, most valuable thing we need and could ever long for: he delights to give us the kingdom. Which is to say, he delights to give us life with him. It makes God happy when he brings us to live under his rule.

Essentially, God is about relationships. He is the Father who loves the Son by the Spirit, *and* he is glad. He is a happy God who is eager to share that happiness with people like us.

GOD IS LOVE

So this is the picture so far: God is a happy Father who has eternally loved his Son in the unceasing fellowship of the Holy Spirit. And there is another truth about God's essence that is inseparable from his fatherhood and gladness. It's that God is love.

The apostle John told us this. In his first letter, writing to assure Christians that God has rescued them, he said, "God is love" (1 John 4:8). Now, to be clear, the word *love* here is not the kind of cute sentiment we might find on greeting cards or the type of love celebrated at a Super Bowl half-time show. My dad used to tell me that *love* is the most under- and overused word in the English vocabulary. We either don't say it enough when we should, or we throw it around too casually. The problem is that we've basically emptied it of any real meaning. In many cases it's become some sort of motivational catchall. But God intends something very different when he gives us this description about himself. "God is love" is deeper than the universe.

And I mean that last sentence with complete seriousness. All hyperbole aside, before there was even a universe, there was God, *and he was a God of love.* But the question is, *Whom* did he love? For this to be real love, it can't be a bland concept; it needs an object. For this love to be essential, it can't be something outside of himself. If God really *is* love, and has been so forever, *whom does he love?*

Answer: *himself.* I mean, his Son.

That's how it works when God is triune.

AN ETERNAL, CREDIBLE LOVE

God loves himself more than anything else because he is the most lovable being there is. It's the right thing to do. If he loves anything else more than he loves himself, he'd be an idolater, because idolatry is esteeming lesser things as if they had ultimate value. And because God is God, he's good and right and true, which means his assessments and ultimate allegiance must always be good and right and true. And all this means, at the very least, that you and I are not the center of the universe. God is.

I remember the first time I stumbled upon this truth. It was like a Copernican revolution for me. I felt like I had found a gold mine. If you would have known me back then, chances are I would have read to you a favorite paragraph or two from the book that guided me in this discovery. (I tend to read to people quotes I'm really excited about.) But see, I had heard all my life that God loved me, and he does. He really does. But I also knew that God was bigger than me, and bigger than anything, and his bigness had to be true in order for his love to actually mean something. His love had to have credibility if it was going to change me. God's supreme love for himself, the supreme, most lovable object, began to connect the dots for me.

But even in loving himself, God's love is a self-giving love for another—namely, the Father's love for his Son. Saint Augustine would jump in here to explain that the Son is the perfect knowledge of God, and therefore the Father loving the Son is the Father loving the perfect knowledge of himself.[3]

The Bible says that this is the reason God does everything he does. God's supreme value is this knowledge of himself, what is often referred to as God's *glory*. God's glory is the shining forth of who God is, and it is so lovable, and so loved by him, that it's as if his love overflows. He wants others to see this knowledge of himself, to behold his glory, and to be drawn into the same vortex of love. At the end of the Old Testament book of Isaiah, God envisions a world where people from everywhere have seen his glory and then go to "the coastlands far away" to, as God says, "declare my glory among the nations" (66:19).

He's all about more people seeing his glory. And this is good news for us, as long as we get the picture right.

To say that God loves himself supremely doesn't mean that he is a cold magnetic block that mindlessly sucks in everything around him. He never checks a "glory box" and then wipes his hands clean. That's not how he works, though we might be tempted to see him that way. Sometimes we're tempted to imagine that if God's love is sovereign, then it must mean his love is disconnected from our lives. But that's not right. When we think *God is love,* we shouldn't let our minds drift off to some "spatially vast entity"[4] or some giant, nebulous blob. Instead, following the Bible's cues, we should see God loving himself as a Father loving his Son and then envision that love spilling over to be shared with others, to be shared with us. God loving God means God the Father esteems the symphony of his fellowship with the Son as the most glorious reality there is, a reality deeper than the universe. The Son is, as Augustine would again add, the perfect knowledge of God himself. And God the Father is passionately devoted to that, *to him.*

God as love is God as a happy Father who enjoys his eternal relationship with his Son by the Spirit. It's the fundamental expression of one God in Trinity and Trinity in unity, whose persons are never blended and whose essence is never divided.

Where It Matters

Taking all these images from the Bible together, we see that God is triune and that his relational character is essentially glad and loving. We might say that God is a happy Father who loves.

But whatever phrase we might use to capture the picture the Bible gives us, the main issue is that first instinctive thought we have.

What immediately comes to your mind when you think about God? What shoots up from your soul to the tip of your tongue when you read the word?

God

What you think about him matters. And what you think about him in that initial take touches you the most. If what you think is shaped by what the Bible says, it's that he is a God who is relational, who is glad, who is love.

This is the God who has laid out a path for us. And it's a path full of significance and happiness.

4

Starting with a Search

> I was trying to find me something but I wasn't sure just what.
> Funny how they say that some things never change.
>
> —Ryan Adams, "Oh My Sweet Carolina"

God is the main character in this story, but by his design he's not the only character. You and I are also here in his world. We humans exist. We breathe, we think, we love, and we crave. Just look around.

We all know we're here, and we know it's important we're here, but then there's a lot we don't know. In many ways we're still our own jungles. There are miles of thick underbrush, towering trunks, and twisted vines, all of which make it hard to pinpoint precisely where we stand on the bigger map. We are sophisticated creatures, and once we start trying to figure ourselves out, it can become quite the expedition. Blaise Pascal can help us navigate this adventure.

SEARCHING FOR SOMETHING

Pascal was born in France in 1623. He was a brilliant mathematician, physicist, philosopher, and theologian (and I've given him the honorific title of *ninja*). Most of what we know about Pascal comes in the form of various notes he left behind. After his untimely death at the age of thirty-nine, his friends searched his house to collect everything he had ever jotted down. They grabbed every notebook and scrap of paper they could find. Once they rearranged and edited them, they published the fragments in a book titled *Thoughts of Mr. Pascal on Religion and on Some Other Topics*. It has since been famously shortened to *Pensées* (French for "thoughts"). The book is equivalent to an archive of modern-day tweets and Facebook updates, except they're from the seventeenth century and they're written by a genius. If we're honest readers, some of his thoughts make no sense. One scholar explained, "Even [Pascal] may not necessarily have remembered the ideas which prompted the jotting down of some key word or phrase."[1] That is to say, although we have a collection of the things he wrote, we don't have a clue about what some of it means, and this makes for a fascinating read. It's like mining. For every seemingly incoherent sentence, suddenly you'll stumble upon a line of pure gold. Consider pensée nineteen: "Man does not know on which level to put himself. He is obviously lost and has fallen from his true place without being able to find it again. He looks for it everywhere restlessly and unsuccessfully in impenetrable darkness."[2]

Pascal's point is that we humans don't quite know what to do with ourselves. On one hand, we know we're special creatures, above dolphins, squirrels, and grizzly bears. We have souls. We came up with the Internet. We make music. But then on the other hand, we know something is missing. We have fallen from our "true place." It feels like we used to be something more than we currently are.

We all know what he's talking about. Everyone, on some level, understands that this world and the people who live here are broken. True, we are surrounded by beauty. There are mountain ranges and waterfalls and zebras. We're able to see these things, to stand on the edge of the Grand Canyon, to smell the sweet aroma of a freshly baked apple pie. But alongside the goodness, seeping through the air of this world's wonder, there is a curse.

I call it the gunk of darkness. Children starve. Tornadoes rip through neighborhoods. Fathers break their promises. Young mothers get breast cancer. Minorities are mistreated. People groups are persecuted. Corruption and oppression, greed and evil—they thrive. Even with all the advancements we've made in the twenty-first century, we humans are still the leading perpetrators of our own victimhood.

But again, the beauty! We can craft into existence amazing works of art, whether in the form of stories or images on a canvas. We have sculpted portraits in the sides of mountains. We have walked on the moon. We have invented cures for all kinds of diseases.

But then again, the darkness! We have birthed Adolf Hitler and others like him. We have vehemently despised one another because of our skin color. We have founded and popularized whole industries that are rooted in the enslavement and exploitation of the vulnerable. We humans, for all our decency, have experienced, seen, and done terrible things to one another. For every good achievement, there are all kinds of examples that show the exact opposite. For every highlight of our progress, there is the dark side of our decline.

"Man does not know on which level to put himself," Pascal said. We see enough that's special about us to know we're something wonderful and enough that's terrible about us to know something has gone wrong. We know we need help. We know we need more.

THAT ORIGINAL GREATNESS

So we keep looking for that original greatness. We want to find that true place. We are glory chasers, in other words—all of us are. We want to rediscover the meaning and depth we know are intrinsic to our being. We recognize, as one author puts it, "Here is not just a body, but a soul. Not just a soul, but a soul with a passion and a desire. Not just a desire for being liked or for playing softball or collecting shells. Here is a desire for something infinitely great and beautiful and valuable and satisfying."[3]

But the problem is that, left to ourselves, we don't know where to find something "infinitely great and beautiful and valuable and satisfying." We're all tuxed up, but we've lost the address of the banquet. We have this appetite for greatness, and we know there are countless signs on the road deceptively promising the fulfillment we want so badly. It's a land full of siren songs, each one luring us somewhere different from where we really want to be.

This is especially the case in societies like ours that encourage individuals to follow their dreams. Other societies in the world with fewer freedoms are too stifling for that kind of rhetoric. People in those societies hunger for depth, but their pursuit of that depth is squelched; therefore, their cultures tend to be creatively anemic and sad.

Thankfully this is not the condition of the modern West, not with its affluence and opportunities. We live in a place and a historical moment where people have never been freer to be and do whatever they want to be and do. It's the culture of "expressive individualism, in which people are encouraged to find their own way, discover their own fulfillment, 'do their own thing.'"[4] The air we breathe tells us to indulge our personal appetites and then let everyone else know about it. Whatever the outcome might be, we all say, "Why don't you be you and I'll be me?"[5]—and we keep singing this line to one another.

This is the cultural situation in which we live, but we know it's not entirely new. Our postmodern, pluralistic sentiments didn't pop out of a vacuum. All our ideas are a response to other ideas, and in most cases we've been through something like it before. The heart of the human condition beats steady. We've always been glory chasers.

ONCE IN CORINTH

We can see glimpses of this in stories of various cultures throughout history, and one of the best places to find these stories is the Bible itself. Take the New Testament, for example, which includes several letters the apostle Paul wrote to actual churches in the first-century world. Some of these letters are considered occasional epistles, meaning they were written in response to specific circumstances in the respective churches. That's the case for Paul's letters to the church in Corinth.

Second Corinthians is Paul's overall response to the distorted mindset of his day. The Corinthian Christians had not yet let the gospel override the influence of their society's value system and way of seeing things, which meant they were pretty much a chip off the old Greco-Roman block. One writer summarized ancient Corinth like this:

> An individual's worth and consequently his respect in the
> community was dependent on the status he was able to proj-
> ect. . . . It was a time when everyone yearned for an admiring
> public. The pursuit of upward mobility thus turned into a quest
> for applause and esteem. . . . When people turned to evaluate
> their contemporaries they looked for the same evidence of
> personal worth and glory that they prized for themselves.[6]

Corinth was a diverse boom city, the perfect mesh of past and present Mediterranean cultures. The Late Greek influence introduced a staunch individualism that stressed a person's ability to determine his or her own worth. Added to this was the Roman emphasis on social classes. The result? Citizens measured their perceived worth in comparison to one another. It was like they were saying "Why don't you be you and I'll be me?"

while they were thinking, *And one of us is better than the other.* It was a society of narcissists who liked to size up their neighbors. It was a world of self-motivated platform builders embedded in a social setting that encouraged each individual to think of himself as better than the one beside him. And this was long before social media.

We can see the Corinthian mind-set in Paul's second letter because of how unimpressed they were with him. From their worldly perspective, Paul was a joke. A lot of them didn't like him. Paul actually quoted his opponents in the letter: "For they say, 'His letters are weighty and strong, but his bodily presence is weak, and his speech of no account'" (10:10). They basically said his writing was decent, but he looked like a clown and wasn't a good speaker.

According to the Corinthian way of seeing things, Paul's persona didn't measure up to their standards. He didn't line up well next to the handsome Greek athletes who competed in their city, and he didn't have a chance beside the eloquent orators who wooed Corinthian crowds. Paul was just Paul, described by at least one ancient account as "a man little in stature, bald-headed, with crooked legs, well-born, with eye-brows meeting and a long nose."[7] But funny as he might have looked, Paul came preaching the gospel. He imparted "a secret and hidden wisdom of God, which God decreed before the ages for our glory" (1 Corinthians 2:7). But the Corinthians couldn't see it.

The Corinthians knew they were made for something big. They were unapologetically on the hunt for glory, but they were looking in the wrong places. They measured greatness by the image they could project and by how others appraised them—*and it was never enough.* Significance for them became about who they were in themselves, defined by what they did, how they looked, and the things they had. Therefore, they stayed hungry. They kept chasing.

Mixed with the Chase

But there is more to say about the Corinthians and their glory chasing. There is always more to say about anyone who pursues self-praise. Just consider what is going on when one person praises another. Say that a Corinthian, or an American for that matter, gets the high five of esteem from his peers. Say that he reaches the top, having leveled the competition and piled up the most respect along the way. He has stepped out, dominated, and now gets the recognition he wanted. What does that glory *do*? How does he cash out all those pats on the back? How does people's approval of him work for him?

It makes him happy.

Pleasure seeking is always mixed into the glory chasing. Pascal wrote,

> "All men are in search of happiness. There is no exception to this, whatever different methods are employed. They all aim for this goal. So while some go to war and others do not, the same desire is in both but from different viewpoints. The will never takes the slightest step except with that aim. This is the motive for men's every action, even those who are going to hang themselves."[8]

We all just want to be happy. It's simple but true. And we feel the gaping loss of our original greatness most acutely, perhaps, by the vexing lack of contentment in our bones. We have this insatiable hole in our souls and nothing seems to fill it. It's like the line from that country song: "We all want what we ain't got . . ."[9]

This is our condition. *In* and *under* and *around* all glory chasing is pleasure seeking. And as far as we might get in pursuing this pleasure in the stuff of this world, whether in the praise of others or the comforts of opulence, we will always come up short. We won't be satisfied.

WE'RE LOOKING SOMEWHERE

You might not feel this way, at least not yet. I recently read somewhere that the people who say money can't buy happiness are typically those who don't have money. And they might have a point. Some extra cash can do a lot in terms of a good night or two, or even a hundred. But the thing is, happiness like that won't last. Cheap thrills, no matter how much you love them, don't last. And as the ancient wise man told us, "[God] has put eternity into man's heart" (Ecclesiastes 3:11). So anything less than eternity won't do.

Seriously, it won't work.

I've been there before. From a bystander's perspective, my own story looks very religious. I grew up in a Christian home and was involved in church my entire life. I was often the kid who spoke up to pray at youth group, and I tried not to cuss when I talked with my buddies. Appearances really matter where I'm from, so I learned how to put on a decent show.

Below the surface, though, in the upside down of my own world, my heart was corroded with restlessness. I assessed my worth by my likability, which meant that I mainly deployed the motions of Christian behavior when I thought it'd win me favor with others. My most loyal conviction was my appetite for the approval of others, not of Jesus. And convictions like that live or die by performance. In order to be liked, I had to perform well in all the categories that my peers valued: sports, machismo, style, girls, morality, religion (yeah, there were all kinds of contradictions). Simple and ordinary as my life was, it was a rat race, and all for what? So people would like me? So I would feel validated?

No matter what I did or whom I impressed, I wasn't satisfied. Anything less than eternity won't do.

It really won't.

Now, I don't mean for this to start sounding like a sermon, but think with me for a minute. Think about your own life and your appetite for the respect of others. I'm guessing everyone wants something like that. There is an honest sense of accomplishment in being recognized for a job well done. Getting things done and getting credit for them creates a buzz. The respect of others feels good. And this is okay. The problem comes when the respect of others is *what you live for*. The problem comes when your desire for people's approval grabs the steering wheel of your work, when the high fives and accolades become the only things that can get you out of bed in the morning. You'll soon discover why this is a problem: because it can't last. It *won't* last. It's not supposed to.

You will never be able to get enough pats on the back, and before too long, someone younger and sharper will take your place. Prominence and popularity are temporary means to satisfy an eternal appetite. Our souls will keep growling. And growling. And growling. We're just *that* hungry. Fame, success, prestige, respect—we're talking about peanuts here. You know that, right? *They're peanuts.*

We're on the search for significance and happiness, with hearts made for eternity, and we just keep popping peanuts.

You know what I'm talking about. Deep down, we all have an inner restlessness. When the energy fades, when your performance wanes, when people get bored talking about you, *what then*? When feelings of regret and failure start coming for your heart with a crowbar, prying and denting and scraping their way inside, *what then*? When you ascend one mountain only to see a hundred more that are higher and farther away than the last, when your lungs can't keep up, when it occurs to you that your heart won't beat forever, *what then*?

Pascal was right. We don't quite know what to do with ourselves. We have this remnant of greatness in our blood, but we don't know what to do with it or where to go. We have this longing for significance and for the happiness that comes with it, but nothing within our reach seems to satisfy it. So we "[look] for it everywhere restlessly and unsuccessfully in impenetrable darkness."[10]

5

Our Enchanted Beginnings

There are no *ordinary* people. You have never
talked to a mere mortal.

—C. S. Lewis

So we have God, and then we have us, the glory chasers and pleasure seekers. Everyone has sensed traces of these two realities. This awareness is deep in us. Every religion, every story, every love—they're all trying to make sense of this situation. And this is where the path paved by the Christian story is like none other. Where other voices might offer advice, admonitions, or a system of strategies and oversimplified resolutions, the God of Scripture speaks up with *news*. It is what the Bible calls the "gospel." The original Greek word means "good news," and whatever you know about it or have heard before, this good news according to Scripture is more comprehensive and beautiful than anything we could have imagined on our own. It starts with this groundwork of significance and happiness.

It's one thing to know that we have this hunger, but we also need to know *why*. What's the story behind our searching? How did it get there?

To Resemble and Reflect

In short, we hunger like we do because God made us this way. This longing in the human soul is there because God created us in his image. God made us great creatures to showcase his great character, and that includes you. *You.*

Stop for a moment and breathe deeply. Those lungs, that pause, this sense—*you.* You were made by God for God. He created you to know and enjoy and reflect and share all the wonders of who he is. The first chapter of the Bible explains,

> Then God said, *"Let us make man in our image, after our*
> *likeness.* And let them have dominion over the fish of the sea and
> over the birds of the heavens and over the livestock and over all
> the earth and over every creeping thing that creeps on the earth."
>
> *So God created man in his own image,*
> *in the image of God he created him;*
> *male and female he created them.* (Genesis 1:26–27)

This sets us apart from every other living thing in the universe. God, the happy Father who has eternally loved his Son in the unceasing fellowship of the Holy Spirit, made us in his image. Theologians have mined the depths of this truth for centuries, and for all the particulars of exactly *how* we reflect God's image, the most powerful point is the most basic: *we are* in God's image. We are images *of him.* And as with any image, our purpose is to resemble and reflect a greater reality. God created us in his image to resemble and reflect him. Just as images exist to point beyond themselves, we humans exist to point beyond ourselves to God.

The purpose of images shouldn't be a surprise to us, and it certainly wasn't to the ancient world in which the Bible was written. Scholar G. K. Beale explained that the practice of ancient Near Eastern kings was to construct statues of themselves in the various territories of their dominion.[1] People knew what it meant when they rode into town and saw in the city square a towering eighty-foot monument of a man. It was a picture of the one in charge. It was a symbol of his authority, of his presence—that he had formerly been there and could drop back in whenever he wanted.

For a more modern equivalent, think of Joseph Stalin, the infamous dictator of the former Soviet Union. As Communism spread throughout Eastern Europe in the first half of the twentieth century, several statues of Stalin were erected in the cities he conquered. You've probably seen pictures of them in school textbooks. The statues were a symbol of Stalin's rule, of just how far his influence had reached. And in many cases, they lasted only as long as his regime was in control. One of the most public expressions of a territory's newfound freedom was to demolish the image. The sculptures were vandalized, smashed, and then removed, and the message of their destruction was that his reign had ended.

Another example (and less maniacal) is the British tradition of disseminating images of the monarch throughout the empire. Even to this day, it is a common practice to see portraits of Queen Elizabeth II everywhere from elementary schools to cricket clubs, from local pubs to the courts of law. On one hand, it's just a picture. But on the other, it is making a statement. One British writer even claims that the images are meant to express a comforting sense of Britain's place in the world.[2] The goal is that citizens be reminded that they are the queen's subjects and that they, in a sense, represent her.

That is sort of what it's like for humans to bear God's image. We are like portraits of God's majesty hung all over the walls of creation. We are images placed throughout the world to represent his rule and presence.

We exist to say that all this is his, that he formed and fashioned us, that he cares about this place, and that he has the ultimate say on how things go. This is what it means that God created us to image him, and this is why glory and gladness are at the root of who we are.

More Than a Statue

It's important to remember that God doesn't intend for us to live as un-affectionate puppets who merely symbolize something about him. We're *like* statues and portraits of his glory, but we're much *more* than statues and portraits. The glory we're created to resemble and reflect is glory that satisfies the deepest longings of our souls. The glory we resemble and re-flect is glory that we've seen, experienced, and enjoyed. The glory that makes us glorious is also the glory that makes us happy. And we would expect nothing less from the God who is himself essentially happy (see 1 Timothy 1:11).

In fact, the topic of happiness is no stranger to the Bible. In the New Testament letter to the Hebrews, the author wrote, "And without faith it is impossible to please [God], for whoever would draw near to God must believe that he exists and that he rewards those who seek him" (11:6).

The author was saying here that our joy in God is as foundational as his existence. If we are going to "draw near to God," we must know, first, that he is real. And second, we must know that he is good—that he will be good for us, enough for us, and worth all costs.

This is the bedrock of every relationship with God. We must believe that he exists and that he makes us happy, that he "rewards those who seek him."

This priority of pleasure shows up other places too.[3] We see it espe-cially in the book of Psalms. In 16:11, speaking to God, the psalmist David exclaimed, "You make known to me the path of life; in your presence there is fullness of joy; at your right hand are pleasures forever-more." In 37:4, he told us, "Delight yourself in the LORD." And check out 40:16, one of my favorite passages:

> But may all who seek you
> > rejoice and be glad in you;
> may those who love your salvation
> > say continually, "Great is the LORD!"

In this verse, David wished, first, that those who seek God would rejoice and be glad in God, and second, that those who love God would praise him. He said the same thing twice but in different ways (which is called synonymous parallelism).

Notice the parallel: Seeking God and loving his salvation coincide. Those who *seek him* and those who *love him* are the same. We can call this human devotion to God.

And then, in the second and fourth lines, we see that this human devotion to God is put in terms of *our pleasure in him* and *our praise of him*. Human devotion to God means that we "rejoice and be glad" in him and that we say, "Great is the LORD!" Those who are *glad in God* and those who *glorify God* are the same. Our experience of resembling and reflecting his glory is inseparable from our joy in him.

The old Westminster Catechism, written in the seventeenth century, says it this way: "Man's chief end is to glorify God, and enjoy him forever." Our purpose for glory *is* our experience of gladness. Or as C. S. Lewis put it, "Fully to enjoy is to glorify. In commanding us to glorify Him, God is inviting us to enjoy Him."[4]

We have a craving for glory because we were made to image God's glory. We have a craving for gladness because we were made to enjoy the glory we image. This is what it means to be human. This is who we are.

Something Special

The psalmist David really got it. In another of his poems, he observed the created world and grappled with our undeniable significance. "When I look at your heavens," he began, "the work of your fingers, the moon and the stars, which you have set in place, *what is man that you are mindful of him, and the son of man that you care for him?*" (Psalm 8:3–4).

David was a man, and as only humans can do, he looked into the starry heavens with reverence.[5] He compared himself to the vastness he could see, and the vastness beyond that, and he felt small. "I'm just a man," he said. But he knew that just a man was still a man, that God made him, and that as a man made by God, he was a little lower than the heavenly beings, which was a high privilege. David knew that God "crowned him with glory and honor" (verse 5).

David knew what we all know. Humans are something special. We carry in ourselves a glimmer of God himself. When we laugh and cry and think, we are saying something about him. To be human is to point beyond ourselves to God's greater reality and to feel the tremors of joy that are part of that pointing, or at least to feel the absence of those tremors and to know they're somewhere around here, somewhere within our reach, or we in theirs. To be human is wonderful like that, and when we look at one another, we should remember this.

The people we encounter day by day are, as C. S. Lewis said, among the "holiest object[s] presented to [our] senses." We are immortals, he said.[6] The people we joke with, the ones we tease, the man who holds a cardboard sign at the corner of Twenty-Sixth and Franklin—we are all enchanted creatures with pedigrees more glorious than a fairy tale could script.

This explains the memory of that "true place" Pascal talks about. This is that depth we've tasted somewhere before. This is that joy for which we long. There is enough that is special about us that we can hear the wonder, but it's like a faint sound in the distance, like the sound a watch might make if it's wrapped in cotton and tucked out of sight, and then some moments its ticking seems to grow louder.

We can hear the wonder, but we also remember what's terrible about us. And there's enough that is terrible about us to know that something has gone wrong. We have smothered the glory and gladness at the heart of our being, and we've hidden it just beneath the floor of the place we live every day.

This is the problem known as sin.

6

Fallen to Where We Are

> Wickedness, when you examine it, turns out
> to be the pursuit of some good in the wrong
> way. . . . Evil is a parasite, not an original
> thing.
>
> —C. S. Lewis

We are meant to be the image of God in the world—you, me, all of us. He made us this way. He spoke us into existence to resemble and reflect the greater reality that he is. But we don't live like it. Something, as we all know, has gone terribly wrong. For centuries, orthodox Christianity has had a name for this. It's called the Fall, and it means pretty much what it says.

The Fall is that part of the story when we humans fell from our "true place." It happened in the beginning of our history when Adam and Eve, our original parents, rebelled against God and brought a curse over our entire race.

This is an intense topic, so my apologies if this chapter comes across like I'm thinking in all caps. I'm not, but I can understand that it might feel that way. The truth is, although everyone everywhere has felt the curse of sin, only the gospel deals with it honestly. The apostle Paul, in another letter found in the New Testament, explained it like this: "For all have sinned and fall short of the glory of God" (Romans 3:23).

We can learn a lot from this one verse. Paul gives us two straight-forward truths: first, sin is everyone's problem; and second, sin has to do with the glory of God.

ALL HAVE SINNED

"All have sinned." There is no gentler way to put it without fudging the facts. Sin caused the Fall; sin is what Adam and Eve did when they turned from God and brought a curse on the rest of us; sin is what we've all done.

That is what Paul meant when he said, "All have sinned." We've all reenacted the fateful actions of our first parents, and therefore, as much as we might like to complain about them and begrudge our depraved inheritance, it's only a matter of time until we realize that *we are them.* It's sort of like how Nietzsche put it: sometimes we tend to become the monsters we gripe the most about. We've all turned from God. We've not only suffered the curse but also participated in it, which might be one of the most misunderstood parts of this whole story.

Everyone knows the word *sin,* and most people know it's not good, but it's rare that we really grasp what the Bible says about it. One theologian goes so far as to say, "One simply cannot make sense of the Bible without a profound and growing sensitivity to the multifaceted and powerful ways the Bible portrays sin."[1]

What exactly is it, then? What does it mean for us to sin?

WHAT DOES IT MEAN TO SIN?

It is easier to talk about the effects of sin than to zero in on the definition of sin itself. That's because the devastation of sin is everywhere around us, and our interaction with the wreckage is more palpable than with the winds that caused it. But it's also because the Bible uses several metaphors to describe sin. We get a buffet of pictures instead of one uniform definition.

When it comes to the metaphors themselves, sin as a burden is the most dominant picture of sin in the Old Testament.[2] By the time of the New Testament, the dominating metaphor begins to shift from a *burden we carry* to a *debt we owe*. There is obvious overlap between burdens and debts, and we can connect with both on a personal level. In one sense, the metaphor of burden is sort of a catchall for several things. Debt, for example, can be a burden, and so can guilt. As a matter of fact, guilt can feel so heavy and burdensome that it eats you alive.

In the Netflix original series *Bloodline,* a good family has done a bad thing. I won't give it away, but in one scene, days after the bad thing was done, a complicit character says to another, "Don't you ever feel guilty?"

The other character replies, "You can't think that way."

The irony of the dialogue, though, is that the guilt-ridden character isn't thinking that way; *he's feeling that way,* and he can't help it. His guilt, his debt, has become an inescapable burden. The show impressively illustrates this theme.

But both the burden and debt metaphors still seem to be talking about symptoms of the problem instead of the problem itself. To get the real sense of sin, we have to drill down beneath the metaphorical concepts. We have to put the array of images together and reflect on them. When we do that, we see two categories emerge. One has to do with failure and the other with rebellion.[3]

The first category gets at our lack, seen in such terms as *lawlessness, unrighteousness, ungodliness, ignorance,* or simply to *fall short,* as Romans 3:23 says. The second category gets at rebellion, which is the active side of things. It's seen in words like *trespass, transgress,* or *disobey.* These are the things we do outright.

Both categories represent different angles on sin, but they're both sin. They share a common darkness. Whether missing the mark and lacking what we shouldn't, or veering off course and barreling out of bounds, sin is always *a willful, personal snub of the God who made us.*

Sin is when we offend our Maker. It's when we attempt to forge a path for ourselves other than the one he has for us. It's when we scoff at his existence and his standards and when we, in our actions, thoughts, desires, emotions, words, or deeds, do anything that displeases God and deserves blame.[4]

And this might be the most misunderstood concept when it comes to sin.

How We Get Sin Wrong

When it comes to how we view sin, the temptation is to make it all about our actions. And when it's all about our actions, the focus becomes our behavior. And when the focus is our behavior, we begin to equate sin strictly with rule breaking. When that happens, we create an environment that makes dos and don'ts the sole basis of a righteous life, and that leads down a dead-end road.

It means either you keep the rules and deceive yourself with a superficial grasp of the human condition, or you conclude that the whole construct is ridiculous and live like hell.

Neither option gets to the heart of the matter.

The self-righteous religious person and the wannabe wolf of Wall Street have that in common. Neither understands that the heart behind our actions matters more than our actions, that our actions are always an indication of our hearts, and that sin has ruined it all. Sin is the willful snub of God, even in our unspoken attitudes, in those moments when no one else is watching, when our sin is too deep for anyone else to witness.

Sin happens in the dark of the night when the nature of our soul itself is an obscene gesture toward God, when we want to run away from the reality of his being, when we want nothing to do with his ways. Sin is both the act *and* the disposition beneath, before, and after the act. It's both *what* we do or don't do and *why* we either do it or don't do it. Sin is the mouthiest of backseat drivers, the one who, as often as we allow it, hurtles over our shoulder, elbows us in the face, and grabs for the steering wheel. Sin in its essence is, as the late theologian John Webster summarized it, the despising of who God made us to be.[5]

And the apostle Paul said that everybody has done this. *Everybody.* He made this point clear. Jew or Gentile, every person from every ethnicity, has sinned. We've not lived up to the purpose for which we were made. "There is no distinction," as Paul put it, "for all have sinned and fall short of the glory of God" (Romans 3:22–23). All of humanity is on level ground, which means sin is everyone's problem. And sin has to do with God's glory.

WE'VE SEEN GLORY

It's not clear what glory has to do with sin until we back up and see how Paul described sin in this same letter to the Romans. There is where we find the most graphic explanation of our sin problem in the New Testament. It's a tightly argued portion of Scripture, each line hanging on to what comes before it, sort of like that barrel of monkeys you played with as a kid.

Paul began with the pronouncement of God's wrath on the unrighteousness of man: "For the wrath of God is revealed from heaven against all ungodliness and unrighteousness of men, who by their unrighteousness suppress the truth" (1:18). He said what we've already seen and know at heart: something has gone terribly wrong with us. We humans, for all our wonder, are also creatures of terror, and God is well aware. Humans are ungodly and unrighteous. We are willfully deficient in those core characteristics that resemble and reflect God, which means we don't image him as we should.

And that is because we have suppressed the truth. We have smothered the knowledge of God in our lives. We've wrapped it in layers of cotton and tried to hide it beneath the floor of our homes. We've tried to muffle the noise, to stop the ticking that grows louder and louder in the stillness of the night.

"Don't get me wrong," Paul would say, "there is indeed a noise we've tried to hide." As he put it, "For what can be known about God is plain to them, because God has shown it to them" (verse 19). Specifically, Paul continued in the next verse, the whole created world is filled with the "invisible attributes" of God's power and presence. The fingerprints of his glory cover the entire planet. Everywhere we turn and look, outside and within, God's glory is there, shining forth, somehow, to tell us about him. Given the wonders of creation, it's harder not to believe in God than to believe.

Yeah, that's right. For everything that casts doubt on faith, there is a steady stream of things that cast more doubt on unbelief. James K. A. Smith said that it's the sign of the times: it's never been harder to believe *and* harder not to believe.[6] God's existence is just too perceptible. There's too much of him out there and too much consciousness of ourselves to make atheism an easy option. The late novelist David Foster Wallace, reflecting on his own struggle with doubt, wrote, "The fact that the most powerful and significant connections in our lives are (at the time) invisible to us seems to me a compelling argument for religious reverence rather than skeptical empiricism as a response to life's meaning."[7]

WE'VE SUPPRESSED GLORY

We find little compelling arguments like this everywhere. God has designed it this way on purpose, and as much as we'd like to get away from it all, we can't. Whether in those things we see or those invisible things we feel deep down inside, *God haunts us.* The noise grows louder and louder, and the only way to live without ripping up the floorboards and getting honest is to suppress the noise more effectively.

So we do, and that leaves us "without excuse" (verse 20).

Paul explained, "For although they knew God, they did not honor him as God or give thanks to him" (verse 21). In other words, although we know there's Someone out there and we're a special kind of species, we have refused to live in a way that befits our mission to image God. Eugene Peterson's paraphrase of verse 21 nails it: "What happened was this: People knew God perfectly well, but when they didn't treat him like God, refusing to worship him, they trivialized themselves into silliness and confusion so that there was neither sense nor direction left in their lives" (MSG).

This is when things really go haywire.

WE'VE SOLD GLORY

"Claiming to be wise," Paul said next, "they became fools, and exchanged the glory of the immortal God for images resembling mortal man and birds and animals and creeping things" (verses 22–23). He said the same thing a couple of verses later: "They exchanged the truth about God for a lie and worshiped and served the creature rather than the Creator" (verse 25). In the blindness of sin, beneath the curse of the Fall, we humans trade in the greater glory of the immortal God for the lesser glory of mortal things. Instead of worshiping the God in whose image we're made, we worship ourselves and the stuff we make.

And God's judgment on all of this, for now, is to let it happen. "God gave them up," Paul repeated three times (verses 24, 26, 28). God says, basically, "Suit yourself," and he lets us go glory chasing and pleasure seeking down all the dead-end roads we prefer. This is all of us, remember. This is the problem of sin, and it's everyone's problem. It leaves us no question why Paul said in Romans 3:23, right after "All have sinned," that we also "fall short of the glory of God."

We've fallen so short of his glory. The original Greek word means "to lack." It's the same word used in the gospel of John just before Jesus turned the water into wine, when the wine "ran out" (2:3). It means we don't have any more. What once was there now is gone.

And it's gone because when we saw the glory, when we perceived the presence of God in this world, we turned our heads and lifted three planks in the flooring. We tried to hide it beneath the hardwood, to suppress it, and then, well, we sold it. We swapped the glory of the eternal God for a fabricated greatness we've forged on our own, one that never seems to be enough. We were created to image God, to resemble and reflect his glory, but we've seen it, suppressed it, and sold it, and now we're left with an emptiness nothing else can fill.

That's the problem of sin. We've gotten rid of the very thing that gives us lasting pleasure.

There is more, though. If we're not imaging *God,* not shining forth his glory, not enjoying the truth of who he is, *what are we doing?* Sin is the willful snub of God that includes both our failure and our rebellion.

So what does that mean for our lives and the world around us?

WE SPEAK SLANDER

Sin means we speak into existence lies about the way things really are.

Sin confuses everything for us. It makes us believe we can reconstruct reality as if God doesn't exist. This is how we've "trivialized [ourselves] into silliness and confusion so that there [is] neither sense nor direction left in [our] lives" (Romans 1:21, MSG). The old Latin phrase captures it: *homo incurvatus in se*—"humanity curved in on itself."[8] It means we're sprinting in circles, stopping every now and then to stare ever so dizzyingly into an abyss of questions—questions we don't want to face but can't stop staring at.

And then, worse even than this, our sin slanders God.

Sin means we tell lies about *him*. Instead of infusing the world with the truth of God's ways, we pollute the world with deceit. We refuse to recognize his worth. We've fallen for what's false, over and over again, as did our first parents. We believe that we humans don't really need God and that he's not nearly as good as he claims (see, we *are* the monsters). That's what the Fall has done. And all of us, all of us fallen and tainted by sin, have conspired in this treason. We've all believed, crawling right into the serpent's scheme: *Yes, God might as well not exist, and yes, he must be holding us back from something better.*

A scene from Scripture helps make the point.

THE BOLD-FACED LIE

In the book of Deuteronomy, God addresses his people about their sin. A long (and fascinating) backstory tells us how the nation of Israel became God's people. But for now, the main thing to know is that God had been wondrously kind to them. The root of his blessing stretches for generations, back to a promise he made to Abraham (who was a nobody God made a somebody by sheer grace).

God had cared for his people ever since that promise. He prospered them in a foreign land and miraculously freed them from ethnic slavery. He made a way for them when there was no way, even splitting an entire river so they could walk through on dry ground. He was serious about Israel being *his people,* the object of his love. He actually called them *Jeshurun,* a Hebrew word that means "upright."

Israel was God's rescued people, a people meant for righteousness, except for the problem known as sin.

How do you think they responded to God's grace and power? Deuteronomy 32:15–18 tells us:

> But Jeshurun grew fat, and kicked;
>> you grew fat, stout, and sleek;
> then he forsook God who made him
>> and scoffed at the Rock of his salvation.
> They stirred him to jealousy with strange gods;
>> with abominations they provoked him to anger.
> They sacrificed to demons that were no gods,
>> to gods they had never known,
> to new gods that had come recently,
>> whom your fathers had never dreaded.
> You were unmindful of the Rock that bore you,
>> and you forgot the God who gave you birth.

Let me paraphrase this very simply: Ancient Israel, in response to God's kindness, became a bunch of ungrateful slobs. They scoffed at God. They didn't merely lose sight of him; they turned their backs, dismissed his presence, and said, with the ugliest tone you can imagine, "Forget you."

They chased after other gods too—fake gods. They sacrificed to demons. They guzzled confusion like it was Gatorade, and they rejected reality like it was a disease. It's as if they tried to forge and inhabit a world where God didn't exist. They became insane and dishonest. They said to God in their defiance, "You cannot give us what we need."

And that's the lie. That's the bold-faced lie.

THE LIE WE'VE SPREAD

Our sin spreads the lie that God cannot fulfill the deepest longings of our hearts. That hunger for glory and gladness we have, that insatiable craving to matter and be happy? Sin tells the whole world that God can't help us. Sin says he isn't enough, that he can't cut it, and so we'd better go search for fulfillment someplace else.

This is why the prophet Jeremiah mentioned two sides of the same coin when it comes to our sinful rebellion. In another Old Testament text, written later in Israel's history, God spoke these words through the prophet:

> Be appalled, O heavens, at this;
> > be shocked, be utterly desolate,
> > declares the LORD,
> for my people have committed two evils:
> they have forsaken me,
> > the fountain of living waters,
> and hewed out cisterns for themselves,
> > broken cisterns that can hold no water. (Jeremiah 2:12–13)

Do you see the two evils? First, they have forsaken God, the fountain of living waters; and second, they have made for themselves cisterns that can't hold water. First, they have abandoned God and said, "He's not enough!" Second, they have looked for fulfillment elsewhere and said, "*This* will do it!"

But no, it won't. A broken cistern can't hold water, especially not the water we're missing. But we keep believing the lies anyway, hoping next time will be different from the last, hoisting up one cistern after the other: *this* will, and again, *this* will, and again, *this* will. But none can hold the water.

We're all, in our sin, searching for the God we've forsaken. As one author put it years ago, even "the young man who rings the bell at the brothel is unconsciously looking for God."[9]

This is you, me, all of us. We're all ringing the bell somewhere. "All have sinned," Paul said. We've all turned away from the God who created us to image his glory, to experience his gladness, and instead we've slandered him and chased after meaning and happiness in the fleeting things around us.

This is what we've done. This is where we've fallen. But we don't have to stay here. God sent someone to rescue us.

7

Jesus

It seemed like some kind of vulgarity the first time I met a boy named Jesus. It didn't matter that the pronunciation was different. When my classmate handed in his fourth-grade homework, written in the top corner of the paper was *J-e-s-u-s*—and that didn't seem right.

It didn't seem right to me that the God my family worshiped could share his name with a kid, just a normal kid like me, with dirty elbows and dried pizza sauce left on his cheek from lunch. How could my friend actually call himself Jesus, or Jesús, or whatever? How could a regular boy, a boy like me, call himself by God's own name?

I am still asking a similar question today, but the words aren't in the same order. Questions work that way, you know. Our basic questions don't change much over time, not the ones about life and God. As much as the words themselves are replaced and certain parts get switched around, we adults don't ask anything entirely different from what we asked as kids. And when it comes to Jesús, my question now isn't how a boy could call himself by God's name, but how God himself could become a boy.

I can still imagine Jesús standing in line, leaving the cafeteria with the rest of our class, still wearing some of the pizza on his face, but the bigger deal to me now is the God who made himself *like* Jesús. That part is the most baffling. God became a human. He became a regular boy, a boy like me, a man like me, a person like all of us.

WELCOME TO THE NEW TESTAMENT

When we open the pages of the New Testament, we find a genealogy. Right from the start we see that Jesus, this baby born in Bethlehem, has an ancestry that traces back to Abraham (see Matthew 1:1–17). This ancestry, Luke tells us in his gospel account, links Jesus inseparably to Adam and the beginning of humanity (see 3:38).

In other words, there is a lot of backstory on Jesus before the Gospels, and it's pretty much the entire Old Testament.

The main thing we should know about this backstory is that God has a people—and has always had a people since he made a promise to Abraham back in the first book of the Bible (see Genesis 12). Thousands of years before Jesus was born, inexplicable apart from God's sheer grace, he came to a man named Abram, a pagan in ancient Mesopotamia, and he told him he was going to bless him, make him into a mighty nation, give him a special place to live, and through his offspring bring good to the entire world (see verses 1–3).

The story of how God does this, through all the ups and downs (mostly downs) of fallen humanity, is what ushers us into the New Testament.

The story of Abram himself, who became Abraham ("father of a multitude," 17:5), is itself full of suspense. Simply put, God made a way when there was no way. That's actually become a song in my house. The story has become such a big deal for us that my kids wrote a little ditty about it. It goes, "God made a way when there was no way," and they just keep singing that line over and over. Because it's true.

God made a way for Abraham, waiting to give him his promised son until he was "as good as dead" (Hebrews 11:12). Then came Isaac, Jacob, and his twelve sons. Jacob's name was changed to Israel (which would become the nation's name), and Israel's sons, including Joseph, through many twists and turns all ended up in Egypt.

While in Egypt the nation multiplied in number, which the new Pharaoh didn't like, so he enslaved them all. They endured years of back-breaking labor, but they continued to grow in spite of it.

Then came Moses, the one called by God to set his people free from slavery. And with Moses came the plagues, the mighty signs and wonders that God brought upon Egypt and its gods.

Then the people escaped from Pharaoh when the Red Sea was split in two, and they were scot-free, except from their own hearts. The people grumbled about the water, about the food, about the leaders, about the God who had liberated them. And so God gave them the Law, which was meant to show them what it looks like for God to be their God and they his people.

But before that was even put into effect, the people were off worship-ing a golden calf, singing and dancing and sacrificing to a statue. The whole thing almost ended right then and there. And it might have if Moses had not prayed and reminded God what he already knew, that his promise to Abraham was on the verge of being destroyed.

After the Law the people wandered in the wilderness, but eventually they journeyed to the Promised Land God had sworn to Abraham. Then Moses died and Joshua took the mantle of leadership, and God continued to do amazing things for his people, starting with the Jordan River, split

right in two. God made a way when there was no way. And then Israel
conquered her enemies and took the land God had promised them.

But those hearts of theirs got them into trouble again.

The cycle of sin, judgment, and repentance repeated itself again and
again, until the people demanded a king and God relented. Of the kings,
the greatest was David, a simple boy from Bethlehem whom God himself
had chosen and to whom God had given a promise reminiscent of the one
to Abraham, a promise of offspring and blessing. This promise was of a
son whose reign would never end, a son of David but a king better than
David, a ruler called the Anointed One: the *Messiah* in Hebrew, the
Christos in Greek, or as we say in English, the *Christ*.

And we keep our eyes peeled at this part in the history.

Who is this son, this Christ? Would it be King Solomon? No, it
wasn't Solomon, nor the son after him, nor the son after him.

The kingdom was divided and more kings came, one after another,
and all of them, good or bad, had one thing in common: they died.

And the people's wickedness worsened to the point that God had to
bring judgment. So he sent prophets to warn Israel and Judah, to tell
them they had to pay for what they'd done, for the ways they had forsaken him and mistreated others.

But the prophets also told them what God was sure to include: that
things would not always be this way, that one day God was going to make
it all right, that he was going to send that son of David, and that he was
going to rescue his people once and for all.

But that was the future.

Judgment was coming nonetheless, and the people became dispos-
sessed, ruled by one foreign power after another until we come to the
Common Era, when the Romans were in charge.

By the time of the Common Era the question had become whether
God was going to make good on those promises to Abraham and David.

People wondered, *Will that Christ come or not? And how should we live until he does?*

CALL HIM CHRIST

Those questions were in the air of first-century Palestine when a young pregnant couple rushed into Bethlehem one night, the woman wincing with contractions. This couple, Joseph and Mary, whose names made it into Matthew's genealogy, had to settle for a stable because the motel was full. And it was there, in that little town, in a stable of all places, that the promised Son was born, the One "who is called Christ" (Matthew 1:16).

The promised Christ had come, Matthew tells us, right in the middle of Israel's mess. He had been born into the thick of their struggle, the struggle of a people, humans like you and me, to trust the God who made them.

Despite what God had said, despite the incredible things he had done in their past, the people of Israel were still like us, glory chasers and pleasure seekers, trying to find a home for the longings of their souls. They couldn't figure it out on their own, which is why they looked for a Savior. And a Savior, indeed, is what the Christ came to be.

CALL HIM JESUS

Before his birth, early in Mary's unexpected pregnancy, an angel came to Joseph to explain more of what was going on with this promised child.

First, and helpfully, the angel made clear to Joseph that the boy growing inside Mary wasn't a typical boy. Joseph knew, at the very least, that this boy wasn't *his*. But this boy, as the angel would tell him, had come from God. The angel continued, "[Mary] will bear a son, and you shall call his name Jesus, for he will save his people from their sins" (verse 21).

The name Jesus comes from the Hebrew name *Yeshua,* which is often translated as "the Lord saves."[1] And *that* was exactly the point: Jesus was named *Jesus* because God had sent him to save his people, and that was the name that stuck. That was his first name. It was a personal name like the names we all have, a name bestowed on him with a purpose by those who gave it to him. The promised Christ had finally come to save his people. So the angel said, "Call him Jesus."

I'm not sure what you think when you think of that name, Jesus.

There is something arresting about it to me. It seems both holy, even eerie, and also plain-as-dirt common. Author Frederick Buechner, in one of my favorite sermons, expressed that feeling of mine perfectly when he talked about what it's like when we stumble across the words *Jesus Saves.* Chances are we've seen them somewhere, on billboards or homemade signs or maybe even tattooed on the back of someone's arm (like the one a friend of mine has). Buechner captured their power:

> There is something in the name "Jesus" itself that embarrasses us
> when it stands naked and alone like that, just *Jesus* with no title
> to soften the blow. It seems to me that the words "Christ Saves"
> would not bother us half so much because they have a kind of
> objective, theological ring to them, whereas "Jesus Saves" seems
> cringingly, painfully personal—somebody named Jesus, of all
> names, saving somebody named whatever your name happens to
> be. It is something very personal written up in a place that is very
> public, like the names of lovers carved into the back of a park
> bench or on an outhouse wall.[2]

Yes, it's something like that. Jesus does save, and it gets to us.

Jesus came to be the Savior of his people, even though he might have been different from what they expected. The salvation Israel needed had seemed obvious, they thought. They were an oppressed people; a foreign governor ruled their land; it didn't feel like the kingdom they once had back in their storied past of God's promises and blessings. They were looking for a Messiah to fix things, to restore the temple to its former prominence, and to defeat the Romans.[3]

But here the angel said that the promised Christ called Jesus had come to save his people *from their sins.* And by that he didn't mean merely the consequences of their sins. Jesus had come to save them from the sins themselves, in their entirety: the failure, the rebellion, every part of them.

CALL HIM IMMANUEL

That is what Matthew, the gospel writer, was saying. He actually chimed in as the narrator before the first chapter ends. "All this," he said—the conception of Jesus, his history, the meaning of his name—

All this took place to fulfill what the Lord had spoken by the prophet:

"Behold, the virgin shall conceive and bear a son,
    and they shall call his name Immanuel"

(which means, God with us). (1:22–23)

Call him *Christ.* Call him *Jesus.* And now, call him *Immanuel* (see verses 16, 21, 23).

Matthew even added a parenthetical explanation because he didn't want us to miss the meaning of this name: "They shall call his name Immanuel *(which means, God with us)."* He wanted us to know that the promised Christ, Jesus, who will save his people from their sins, is also *God with us,* God right here among us.

Right from the start, before we can affirm much else about Jesus, we see that he, this baby related to Abraham and David, is *Christ,* is *Jesus,* is *Immanuel.* He is the promised Messiah, the One who has come to save us, God right here among us.

CALL HIM THE BELOVED SON

In the third chapter of Matthew's gospel, at Jesus's baptism, we learn more details about what it meant that Jesus was God with us. The boy Jesus had grown into a man, and at the scene of his baptism, on the banks of the Jordan River, he was about to launch his earthly ministry. But this would not have been a jaw-dropping scene, at least not right away, since John the Baptist had been baptizing folks for days. A multitude of people in the area had already stood in the Jordan River with him. There was probably a crowd there the day Jesus was baptized.

Imagine that for a minute, a crowd of people gathered near a river, and Jesus standing in line like all the others, looking like everyone else, waiting for his turn.

John the Baptist knew Jesus was unique, but no one else knew, not until the moment of his baptism. Then came the revelation: "When Jesus was baptized, immediately he went up from the water, and behold, the heavens were opened to him, and he saw the Spirit of God descending like a dove and coming to rest on him; and behold, a voice from heaven said, 'This is my beloved Son, with whom I am well pleased'" (verses 16–17).

It's hard to say what you would have done if you had been there and seen that. It's a lot to take in. The guy standing in front of you in line, the guy who looks a lot like you, whose elbows might have even been a little dirtier than yours, *that* guy gets a bird on his shoulder and a voice from heaven.

As readers, we have an advantage. It's not quite as jolting for us. That dove, as Matthew tells us, symbolizes the Spirit of God. That voice, which we'll hear again in Matthew's gospel, is God the Father's (see 17:5). And what it tells us about Jesus, who appeared to be just another guy with dirty elbows standing in line, is that he is someone special. What we learned about him through his names we now see in his baptism: that the promised Christ, Jesus come to save us, is God with us *as God's Son*.

If you've been in Christian churches, you've heard that Jesus is the Son of God, but still, whether you've heard it before or not, none of us should breeze past this truth. The apostle John gives us more background in his gospel account. It's actually how he opens in 1:1–3: "In the beginning was the Word, and the Word was with God, and the Word was God. He was in the beginning with God. All things were made through him, and without him was not any thing made that was made."

From the beginning, John said, back before anything else, there was the Word: *with* God and *himself* God.

John's introduction refers to the essence of God as triune, that God is the everlasting Father who has eternally loved his Son in the unceasing fellowship of the Spirit. "We worship one God in trinity and the trinity in unity," says the Athanasian Creed, "neither blending their persons nor dividing their essence." Each person of the Trinity is distinct, and yet each is equally God, sharing in "majesty coeternal." And John said the eternal Son of God is the Word.

This recalls Augustine's commentary on the Son of God being the perfect knowledge of God. The Son of God is the perfect resemblance of who God is, and as the Word, the Son is that resemblance beamed out for others to see. That's what words do, after all. They say something. They reflect meaning. The eternal Son, then, as the Word, possesses and expresses who God is, and he does it so perfectly that he himself could be called the glory of God. He's the very embodiment of it. That is what it means to be the divine Word, to be the eternal Son of God.

And it was this eternal Son who became *man,* born into this world as the promised Christ, Jesus come to save us, God right here among us. He came to perfectly show us who God is. John said it like this: "And the Word became flesh and dwelt among us, and we have seen his glory, glory as of the only Son from the Father, full of grace and truth" (1:14).

THAT NIGHT ON THE SEA

Several chapters after Jesus's baptism in the gospel of Matthew, we come across a pivotal scene when the disciples themselves recognized who Jesus is.

It comes in Matthew 14, after a long day of ministry for the disciples. They had hosted dinner outside for over five thousand people. Aside from the organizational demands of it all and the relational toll of looking over five thousand souls in the eyes as they handed them dinner, these disciples had been hit with the adrenaline high of seeing the two fish and five loaves they scrounged up become hundreds of fish and hundreds of loaves. They had to be tired and mesmerized.

But once the crowds were finally dismissed, Jesus told the disciples to get into their boat and leave. He was going off to pray alone until later that night when he would rejoin them.

He did rejoin them later, when the disciples were farther out in the water, not only exhausted but also beaten by the wind and waves. Matthew tells us, "And in the fourth watch of the night he came to them, walking on the sea" (verse 25).

Once again, it's hard to say what you would have done if one night you saw someone walking on water toward you, a man or woman like yourself, who might have had dirty elbows every now and then and who, at least if he ate in a hurry, could have had a little lunch left on his face. It's a lot to take in. The disciples were terrified, until Jesus spoke.

Immediately Jesus said to them, perhaps upon hearing their cries of fear, "Take heart; it is I. Do not be afraid" (verse 27).

They weren't even sure it was him yet when Peter, Jesus's most outspoken disciple, grisliest with his faith, wanted to jog out on the sea to meet him. You've probably heard the story. Peter stepped out on the water, he walked, he sank, he screamed for help, and then Jesus got them both to the boat safe and sound.

Once they were both in the boat, with all the disciples standing around, the wind and waves ceased. Peter was soaked, Jesus was dry, and the other disciples were mystified again by what their tired eyes had seen.

They then did what any of us would have done.

"And those in the boat worshiped him, saying, 'Truly you are the Son of God'" (verse 33).

THE WORSHIP OF ONE

The disciples called Jesus, this man like them, like you and me, the Son of God—*and they worshiped him.*

The disciples knew "there is only One who can command the wind and storm, only One who can stride across the waves," and in that boat, bowing before Jesus, the disciples acknowledged that Jesus was that One.[4]

From Matthew's perspective, it was a really big deal that the disciples did this, since Matthew was among them. Matthew remembered, better than we do, that earlier in his gospel, in chapter 4 when Satan tempted Jesus, Jesus quoted Deuteronomy 6:13: "It is the LORD your God you shall fear. Him you shall serve." The heart of this verse, and Jewish theology as a whole, was that their God—the one, true God who had created the world and made a covenant with Israel—*was the only God.*

YHWH (pronounced YAH-way) was the personal name that God gave himself earlier in the Old Testament (see Exodus 3:13–14). That personal name (and its spelling) is known as the *tetragrammaton* (meaning "four letters"). Even to this day Jewish people, out of reverence, do not pronounce the name with vowels (instead they refer to God as *Adonai,* which means "Lord"). If the name is ever written, it gets transliterated from the four Hebrew consonants as YHWH, which our English Bibles translate as "Lord" (typically in small caps).

The Jews of Jesus's day firmly believed that there was only one God, that his name was YHWH, and that YHWH alone should be worshiped. They asserted that two key passages of Scripture taught this truth, passages they recited during the morning and evening of every day.[5] They were Exodus 20:2–6, the first two commands of the Ten Commandments, and Deuteronomy 6:4–6, known as the Shema, which begins, "Hear, O Israel: The Lord our God, the Lord is one" (verse 4).

The Shema comes in the section of Deuteronomy that Jesus quoted when he was tempted to worship Satan (see Matthew 4:9–10). Without a doubt Jesus knew that YHWH alone is God and that YHWH alone should be worshiped. The disciples knew this too, which is what makes the scene in that boat so fascinating.

After the wind and waves had ceased, the disciples *worshiped Jesus,* and Jesus received it. Jesus said in Matthew 4 to worship only YHWH, and then in Matthew 14 *he accepted the disciples' worship of him.* In seven other scenes in Matthew's gospel, people came to Jesus in the posture of worship and none were rebuked.[6]

Add to this the things that Jesus claimed for himself in the Gospels, for example in Matthew 12:6 when he said, "Something greater than the temple is here," which means Jesus considered himself superior to the presence of YHWH represented at the center of Jewish life. Or consider Matthew 24:35, when Jesus said, "Heaven and earth will pass away, but my words will not pass away." Here Jesus said about himself something that had been said only of YHWH. The prophet Isaiah tells us, "The grass withers, the flower fades; *but the word of our God will stand forever*" (40:8, NRSV).

One author explained, "If we ask ourselves who might legitimately say such a thing [as Jesus did], once again there can be only one answer: we find ourselves face-to-face with the God of the Old Testament."[7]

The promised Christ, Jesus come to save us, God right here among us, eternally beloved Son of the Father, was, to be more precise, *YHWH himself become a man.*

HOLDING THE WHOLE FACT

We can look away from all that's said about Jesus, I guess. We can try to ignore the evidence. But there is no space for us to think that the Gospels, and the entire Bible for that matter, are saying anything other than that Jesus is God.

The hardest part, in my opinion, is not discerning what the biblical witness is getting across, but holding it all together. We're supposed to hold together that Jesus was (and is) eternal God and that he was (and is) also a man, a human like you and me. This is what T. F. Torrance calls the "whole fact" that confronts us in the New Testament.[8] Jesus wasn't a man who became God, but rather he was God who became man, and he lives right now as both fully God and fully man.[9]

Certain thinkers over the centuries have sometimes veered from this "whole fact" into confused fragmentations. Either they've mistaken Jesus as originally human, created like the rest of us but having achieved deity by some kind of divine connection; or they've mistaken Jesus as not really human at all because his deity wouldn't allow such a thing and have concluded that he must have been some kind of a demigod, like an angel.

Neither of these fragmented beliefs has endured, though, after being brought under the Bible's scrutiny and the commonly held conviction of Christians over history.

Jesus—the promised Christ, the Savior come to save us, God right here among us, the Father's eternally beloved Son—*was and is both fully God and fully man.* And it's only when we see him as he truly is that he brings any hope to our stories of longing and brokenness, of glory and gladness.

The God who had promised the Christ was the One who became him. The God from whom we were separated became the Savior to bring us back. The God who created humans to resemble and reflect his glory became a human to do it himself.

True Humanity

Jesus was the perfect image of God, the truest human to ever live, which is exactly what we needed. Israel needed a Savior who could be the Israel they failed to be. We all needed a Savior who could be human in a way that *we fail to be.*

Therefore, Jesus came.

To a world full of sinners, he came.

To individuals created to resemble and reflect God's glory but don't, he came.

To broken people, all of us who are craving the significance we lack and longing for a joy nothing seems to satisfy, he came.

We weren't going to get there ourselves; that part was clear enough. If things were going to be different, it could happen only by God becoming man and doing it himself.

So he did. Jesus came.

Jesus is "the image of the invisible God," Paul said later in the New

Testament (Colossians 1:15). Another writer said, "He is the radiance of the glory of God and the exact imprint of his nature" (Hebrews 1:3). When Jesus came here he brought all of who he is into this world as a human to save us from our sins. The salvation we needed wasn't mere acquittal. We needed more than a pass. We needed a whole new humanity, not one like that of Adam, who turned from God and brought the curse, but a humanity reconciled to God, a humanity united to God in the relationship he intended from the beginning, one of enjoying and resembling and reflecting his glory.

So Jesus came, and he did *that*.

As the beloved Son, he had eternally possessed and expressed God, and then, as God become man, as the promised Christ, as Jesus come to save us, as God right here among us, he resembled and reflected God as his perfect image in human flesh.

Jesus even said that to see *him* was to see *God* (see John 14:9).

He stepped into this world in which we live, all of us, dirty elbows and pizza sauce left on our faces, and he was the human we couldn't be, dirty elbows of his own, lunch on his own face, tempted in every way we've been tempted yet never sinning (see Hebrews 4:15). Where we failed, he thrived. Where we marred the message of God's glory, Jesus resembled and reflected it with power.

There is enough greatness like this in Jesus that he gets our attention, and there is something about him getting our attention, about that double take that happens within our souls, that makes him feel like home, like an echo of the glory and gladness for which we were made.

Jesus, the promised Christ, Jesus come to save us, God right here among us, the eternal Son who is fully God and now fully man—he lived *and lives* as truly human in our place.

And he saves us from our sins.

8

The Violent Rescue

The world's religions have certain traits in common, but until the gospel of Jesus Christ burst
upon the Mediterranean world, no one in the
history of human imagination had conceived of
such a thing as the worship of a crucified man.

—Fleming Rutledge

There is a story in the Old Testament of an epic showdown between
God's prophet Elijah and 450 prophets of the false god Baal.

The scene takes place in the book of 1 Kings, which would have been
in the mid-800s BCE. The nation of Israel was so ravaged by idolatry
that they barely resembled anything close to God's chosen people. Israel's
king was a man named Ahab, and he was a bad king. He had replaced the
worship of God with the worship of Baal, and he had killed all the prophets of God, all except for Elijah, who was in hiding. The question for Israel in those days was whether they would continue to worship Baal or
return to the true God. Elijah was determined to find out.

So one day he stepped out from hiding to arrange a contest with
Ahab and the false prophets. Everyone had gathered at Mount Carmel,
where Elijah came to meet them. "Here's the deal," he said. "We each take

a bull and prepare it as a sacrifice. We put it on the altar. We step back. We pray for fire to come down from heaven. Whichever higher power answers the prayer is the true God, either YHWH or Baal."

The prophets complied and went first. They put a bull on the altar and began asking Baal to send some flames. They did this from morning to noon, but nothing happened. Then noon came and went, "but there was no voice, and no one answered" (18:26). Then they increased the intensity of their plea.

All 450 prophets began limping around the altar and wailing. Then they began to cut themselves. The Bible tells us that they sliced their bodies with swords "until the blood gushed out" (verse 28), still limping, still wailing, desperate to hear something from Baal.

The day dragged on past midafternoon, "but there was no voice. No one answered; no one paid attention" (verse 29). It was a complete failure. Baal was a no-show.

But then it was Elijah's turn. He started by drenching the altar with water. He tried to make it as wet and unlikely to spark a fire as possible. Then he prayed to YHWH, the true God. Fire immediately fell from heaven and consumed the whole sacrifice. The people fell on their faces in true worship. Showdown over.

It was a stunning victory for Elijah, and it makes for a riveting episode in the Bible. But it's still hard for me to get past the sad scene of those false prophets.

Could you imagine anything more gruesome? There were 450 prophets, each of them exhausted, limping and wailing around an altar, gashes on their bodies, blood gushing out, praying to a god who didn't exist. They were desperate to hear the slightest little peep from him. Something? *Anything!* They would have settled for the smallest sign, but there was nothing. There was nothing because there was no one. It was tragic: they had put their bleeding hope in a god who wasn't real.

JESUS FOR US

The Christian story isn't afraid of the dark. Right at the center of the whole thing is death, the most horrible death of the truest human to ever live. Not only did Jesus walk in our shoes, resembling and reflecting God's glory perfectly, but he also stood in our place condemned, slain as a criminal although he was an innocent man.

That part is outrageous enough to make us recoil but too serious to be dismissed. Any attempts to downplay the crucifixion of Jesus simply reflect how watered down American Christianity has become, a Christianity, as Fleming Rutledge calls it, "packaged as inspirational uplift—sunlit, backlit, or candlelit."[1]

Jesus lived a life purer than anything we could imagine, and he died a death darker than we'll ever grasp. And he did both to save us. Both Jesus's living and his dying were for us, to save us from our sins. Theologians have long identified these two parts of Jesus's saving mission as his active obedience and his passive obedience.

In the first part, in his active obedience, the emphasis is on Jesus's righteous life. He stepped forward and blazed the trail for a new humanity, one that fulfilled God's original intention for humans to image and enjoy him. Unlike Adam whose sin brought death, Jesus was the sinless human whose vicarious faithfulness brought life (see Romans 5:18).

Then in the second part, in his passive obedience, the emphasis is on Jesus's sacrificial death. Not only did he epitomize a heart devoted to God, but he also yielded his life to die for sinners. He charted a new way of life, *and* he laid his life down (see John 15:13). He was steadfast in all the ways we weren't, *and* he let himself pay the debt we owed (see Philippians 2:8).

In his active obedience, Jesus lived to resemble and reflect the glory of God. In his passive obedience, Jesus died to reveal God's character and reconcile us to him. And in both, in his work of resembling and reflecting *and* of revealing and reconciling, Jesus gave himself for us.

Both parts were for us, but it's his dying that takes center stage in the story. "His death," Rutledge wrote, "far from being an unfortunate error or derailment of his purpose, was the willed culmination of that life of self-giving for our good."[2] It was his death, that "willed culmination," that makes all the difference. That's the horror to which his holy life trended and where the worst darkness set in.

Your Worst Nightmare

We all are afraid of something. Fear is a powerful force in the human experience that spans all cultures and ages. It doesn't matter where we are or how old we might be, there is always something to scare us.

I went through a stretch as a young kid when I was terrified to go to bed at night. I think it had something to do with watching the first *Ghostbusters* movie. I would leave my lamp on as long as I could, barricade myself behind a wall of stuffed animals, and pull the covers over my head—anything to protect me from the threats my imagination invented. I laugh about it now, but I didn't then. I remember it well enough to this day that I have a special sympathy for my kids when they have nightmares. It doesn't matter how irrational my fears were when I was a kid or how irrational my kids' fears might be now; the feeling of fear as it happens is always *fear*. And fear is powerful, for all of us.

We all can imagine scenarios that horrify us. The question is what creates that fear. What is it that scares you the most?

If you were to think long enough about it, you could probably list several things. And as legitimate as our grown-up fears might be, none of them are the scariest things imaginable, unless you would say you're most afraid of the wrath of God. The hands-down most horrific reality out there is that God is angry at us. And ironically, this most horrifying fear is actually *the most rational*. Again, this might seem a little heavy, but hang in there with me.

Contrary to our popular sentiment, the Bible tells us that God gets angry. Psalm 7:11 says that he is "a God who feels indignation every day." In another psalm, the poet, reflecting on Israel's history and their grumbling against God in the wilderness, reminds us, "Therefore, when the LORD heard, he was full of wrath; a fire was kindled against Jacob; his anger rose against Israel" (78:21). A little later in the Old Testament, the prophet Nahum explained, "The LORD is a jealous and avenging God; the LORD is avenging and wrathful; the LORD takes vengeance on his adversaries and keeps wrath for his enemies" (1:2).

Some well-meaning folks might want to jump in here and say something like "This picture of God is no longer operative." They would try to convince you that God has really turned himself around by the time we get to the New Testament, that he doesn't get angry like that "primitive" vision of him suggests.

But the problem with saying this is that it just doesn't hold up to what the New Testament actually says.

Jesus, meek and lowly as he was, fiercely confronted the self-righteous religious people of his day (see Matthew 23:27; Mark 3:5). He preached woes of judgment against morally obstinate cities like Chorazin and Bethsaida (see Matthew 11:21). When he encountered the oppressive misuse of the temple, he turned over tables and cracked a whip to chase out the swindlers (see John 2:14–17).

Then there is the topic of wrath in Paul's New Testament letters. He says right away in Romans, as we saw earlier in chapter 5, that "the wrath of God is revealed from heaven against all ungodliness and unrighteousness of men" (1:18). Paul even says that Jesus himself will return one day to finally and fully execute the divine anger, "inflicting vengeance on those who do not know God and on those who do not obey the gospel" (2 Thessalonians 1:8).

If we take the Bible seriously, we can't get away from the anger of God. The question for us becomes how that anger fits into the vision of God as essentially relational, happy, and loving. If God really is a happy Father who has eternally loved his Son in the unceasing fellowship of the Holy Spirit, in what way can he ever be angry?

THE LOVE IN ANGER

This question has to do with what anger is. Anger is not an original emotion. It never exists on its own; instead, anger is reactionary and always depends upon a context of previously established love. It can happen only as a reaction to a threat against someone or something we truly value. In fact, the more we consider it, we begin to see that anger itself serves as a form of love that aims to defend our beloved.[3] In human terms, we know exactly how this works.

When the sandwich-shop delivery car comes speeding down my street, my heart rate goes up and my ears start to tingle. I get angry. And I call the store to let them know how important it is that their drivers slow down. The reason I do this, though, is because my children and their friends play by the street in our front yard. They ride their bikes and scooters to one another's houses. They shoot baskets in the driveway. When a car flies down our block at twice the speed limit, my children and their friends are put in danger. And as a parent, I get angry when my children and their friends are put in danger *because I love my children and their friends.*

If you look carefully, behind anger there is always love—and that includes our unjust anger too. Many times we get angry about petty things, which can be traced back to disordered affections. Basically, whatever riles us up exposes what we really care about. It's the same with God's anger, except unlike us, his anger is always righteous because his love is always pure.

The love of God is a gloriously deep topic and so much could be said about it, but the main thing to know is what we saw in earlier chapters: God loves his glory supremely; God loves humans like us whom he created to enjoy, resemble, and reflect his glory; and sin is the full-out assault against this, *against what God loves.*

Sin is our willful, personal snubbing of God. It's when we see his glory, but instead of enjoying and resembling and reflecting it, we belittle it and suppress it and exchange it for the trifles of the world around us. Sin causes us to spread lies about God and separate ourselves more and more from what gives us lasting significance and joy. It defames God's glory and debases ourselves, which means it sabotages the objects of God's affection. And that makes God angry.

But it's not an arbitrary, capricious kind of anger that flies off the handle for no good reason. It's a calculated, deliberate kind of anger that defends what God loves and what sin desecrates: his glory and our everlasting joy.[4] As one theologian summarizes it, the wrath of God is "the determined, willed, chosen, visceral reaction of a holy God against all that dishonors him, rebels against him, and calls him into question."[5] Because of God's love, and because of what sin is and does, God's anger is his response to sin. As long as there has been sin, there has been his wrath.

MERCY AND JUSTICE

We can see this in one of the most important passages in the Bible, Exodus 34.

Moses had just led the people of Israel out of slavery in Egypt. In the short time of his leadership, he had already seen incredible things. He had seen God's miraculous provision and the people's stiff-necked idolatry. He had seen God's grace, and he had seen God's wrath, and in a riveting scene when Moses was praying, he asked to see God's glory.

In one sense, he had already seen God's glory. He had a remarkable relationship with God, so much so that we're told "the LORD used to speak to Moses face to face, as a man speaks to his friend" (Exodus 33:11). But in this moment of prayer, Moses needed God's assurance that he'd be with his people. "Please show me your glory," Moses prayed.

And God answered him.

God told Moses, "I will make all my goodness pass before you and will proclaim before you my name 'The LORD'" (verse 19); that's that Hebrew name YHWH, God's personal name.

So early the next morning Moses climbed to the top of the mountain and waited, all alone, until God came. Then we read that God

> descended in the cloud and stood with him. . . . The LORD
> passed before him and proclaimed, "The LORD, the LORD, a
> God merciful and gracious, slow to anger, and abounding in
> steadfast love and faithfulness, keeping steadfast love for thou-
> sands, forgiving iniquity and transgression and sin, but who
> will by no means clear the guilty." (34:5–7)

This is a big deal in the Bible because God is telling us in a straight-forward manner who he is. He is revealing himself so that he can be trusted. He is letting us know what we should expect from him in the way he deals with sinners like us. In summary, God says that he is both merciful and just, that he forgives sin *and* punishes the guilty.

God is love, so he is merciful and gracious; he's not an ornery, discon-nected deity who's prone to criticize. He is abounding and overflowing in *steadfast love,* the kind of love that can be trusted, that means he always does what he says he'll do.

But because God is love, he responds in anger toward sin. He doesn't let it go. He doesn't sweep it under the rug. Sin has polluted the universe with lies about who he is, and it has wrecked the true happiness of humans created to image him. Sin, *because God loves,* must be punished for what it is and what it does. But how?

How does this God who is essentially loving, who has revealed himself as merciful and just, show mercy and punish sin?

WE SEE BY THE CROSS

This is the question that brings us to one Friday afternoon many years ago, just outside the city walls of Jerusalem.

Each of the gospel writers identified the place as Golgotha, which means "place of a skull." It is the place where Jesus died. It's where Jesus revealed to sinners the character of God and reconciled sinners to God forever.

In one sense, Jesus's entire life was the revelation of God. That is what it means to be the glory of God and to perfectly resemble and reflect that glory in human flesh (see Colossians 1:15). In all that he did, he showed us what God is like, which is why he could say, "Whoever has seen me has seen the Father" (John 14:9).

But it was by his death that he definitively revealed God to us.[6] This was the vivid display, the feature presentation, the loud, unmistakable declaration of this God who had told Moses he is merciful and just.

God revealed to Moses who he is when he descended in a cloud and proclaimed his name on the mountain. God revealed to all of us who he is when Jesus carried his cross up the hill of Golgotha and died in our place. The death of Jesus is the place where we see God, who is both merciful and just, *show mercy and punish sin.*

The apostle Paul made this point clear. In Romans 3:24–26, he wrote that sinners "are justified by [God's] grace as a gift, through the redemption that is in Christ Jesus, whom God put forward as a propitiation by his blood, to be received by faith. This was to show God's righteousness, because in his divine forbearance he had passed over former sins. *It was to show his righteousness* at the present time, so that he might be just and the justifier of the one who has faith in Jesus."

These words are at the heart of the good news.

God forgives sinners and declares them righteous by grace. *It is a gift.* And he gives this gift through the self-sacrifice of Jesus for sinners. That is what Paul meant when he said that God put Jesus forward "as a propitiation by his blood" (verse 25). He was talking about the cross where Jesus died. Paul said that the cross was the place where God *showed us his righteousness:* "This [the cross] was to show God's righteousness, because in his divine forbearance he had passed over former sins" (verse 25).

In other words, over the years there had been a lot of sin that angered God, but he had put up with it. He set it aside and temporarily let it be, holding back his anger until the cross. But Jesus's death was where God punished that sin, where he showed himself to be righteous: the God "who will by no means clear the guilty" (Exodus 34:7). The cross blares at us the justice of God.

Then in Romans 5:6–8, Paul wrote, "For while we were still weak, at the right time Christ died for the ungodly. For one will scarcely die for a righteous person—though perhaps for a good person one would dare even to die—but *God shows his love for us* in that while we were still sinners, Christ died for us."

It's important we know that Jesus died for us when we were ungodly.

We were the least deserving of the slightest favor. We were still snubbing God, spreading lies, swapping the glory of God for ridiculous fillers. We must know this.

And we must also know that a person dying for someone else is the most uncommon kind of self-sacrifice. People don't go around every day dying for other people, even if they're good people, but especially if they're ungodly like us. That's what Paul was saying.

But Jesus died for us *while we were sinners.* Jesus performed the most uncommon form of self-sacrifice for the least deserving people. It is just unheard of. It makes no sense. And the reason Jesus did this was to show us the love of God. The cross blares at us the love of God.

So according to the apostle Paul, when Jesus died on the cross, God showed us his justice *and* he showed us his love. In his dying, Jesus vividly, loudly, unmistakably revealed to us that God is both merciful and just. He forgives sinners and punishes sin.

HE TOOK OUR PENALTY

Paul tells us that Jesus's death showed us this, but now the question is *how.*

In what way does the death of Jesus show us that God is merciful to forgive sinners and just to punish sin? Why does Jesus's dying on the cross do that?

This question gets at the nature of atonement, which is a theological term that refers to how God deals with sin. It gets at what Jesus was actually doing *for us* when he died. To be sure, Jesus accomplished several things in his death, such as leaving us an example (see 1 Peter 2:21) and triumphing over Satan (see Colossians 2:15), but the most important thing he did was suffer in our place for the punishment we deserved as sinners.[7] This is often called penal substitution, which means that Jesus took the penalty of our sins as our substitute.

This is a theme that taps into the ancient sacrificial system of the Old Testament. In fact, when Paul talked about Jesus's death in Romans 3, he used a keyword found several times in the Old Testament. It's the word translated "propitiation."[8]

Paul used this word when he said that God put Jesus "forward as a propitiation by his blood" (verse 25). Propitiation is the sacrificial act by which someone becomes favorable.[9] It's not a very popular word in our day. For one, it doesn't exactly roll off the tongue. Language tends to simplify itself, and I think that's partly why we've kept this clunker out of the English vernacular for centuries. But also, at least in recent years, there has been a backlash against the whole idea that Jesus really suffered sin's penalty in our place, especially if it meant that he suffered God's wrath.

For some, it just seems too grotesque that God would even have wrath and even worse that he'd dish out that kind of punishment. It's too difficult to see how a God who is love can also feel anger (although, as we saw earlier, the two are inseparably connected). As much as I sympathize with the desire to "protect" God's reputation for modern folks like ourselves, the thing to remember is that nobody just made this up. The word *propitiation* is in the Bible, and that means we should pay attention to it.

The first thing to say is what *propitiation* does not mean.

Propitiation, in the Christian sense, is not man's attempt to placate an angry deity. It doesn't mean that sinners like us are left to sacrifice ourselves in order to appease heaven. That was the way some ancient pagans used the word, but that's not how the Bible uses it.[10] In the Bible, in the Christian sense, propitiation is not the works of sinful humans to absorb God's wrath, but it's the work of God himself to absorb his own wrath toward sinful humans.

God was the One who *made* the propitiation. He was the One who initiated this thing, moving toward us in love. It was all his idea, flowing from his sheer mercy. And more than that, not only was God the One who made the propitiation, but he himself, in the person of Jesus, *was* the propitiation.

God satisfied his anger by substituting himself as the one who suffered it: self-satisfaction by self-substitution.[11] He made the sacrifice of himself to satiate his anger.

INTO THE DARKNESS

Jesus became a human like us, perfectly imaging God in all the ways we didn't, and then he went to the lowest, most violent depths to rescue us. He deferred all the rights and comforts we would expect to be afforded to the truest human to ever live, and then "he made himself nothing," even to the point of "death on a cross" (Philippians 2:7–8, NIV).

Jesus died, as God in human flesh, quenching the divine fury against sinful humans by gulping it down in our place. He suffered his own justice against sin by coming to earth "to be sin for us" (2 Corinthians 5:21, NIV), standing condemned in our stead for all the ways we have personally, willfully snubbed *him*. That is what it means when the Bible says that Jesus died for us. Rather than us being punished for our sins, Jesus was punished for our sins. For my sins and for yours.

Stop for a minute and think about that. *Your* sins.

You know about your life. You know how badly you want to matter, how badly you want to be happy. And you know how desperately you've chased after this meaning and happiness in all the wrong places. You know, like I do, how easily we have swapped God for all the trifles around us. You, me, all of us—we've run hard down every dead-end road, shaking our fists at heaven, spreading lies about him in this world, cherishing in our hearts the things we believed would give us what only God can.

All that sin, sin you know and sin you don't—Jesus died for it.

He died as a punishment for you. *You.*

And there, at the place of a skull, when Jesus did that, is where everything went dark, the darkest of dark.

It was dark enough that time in 1 Kings when we saw 450 men exhausted and limping around an altar, gashes all over their bodies, blood gushing out, praying to a god who didn't exist.

But on that Friday at Golgotha, we see the truest man to ever live, the God become man, exhausted and hanging on a cross, gashes all over his body, blood gushing out, dying for sinners who have despised him, sinners like us who wanted nothing to do with him.

That was the darkest moment in history, and Jesus went into that darkness to bring us home.

He, the blessed One, was cursed for us, so that we might be blessed (see Galatians 3:13). He, the sinless One, became sin for us so that we might know his salvation (see 2 Corinthians 5:21). He, the righteous One, suffered for the unrighteous so that he might "bring us to God" (1 Peter 3:18).

9

He Didn't Stay Dead

In the Christian story God descends to re-ascend.
He comes down; down from the heights of absolute being into time and space, down into humanity . . . down to the very roots and sea-bed of the
Nature He has created. But He goes down to
come up again and bring the whole ruined world
up with Him.

—C. S. Lewis

So Jesus died.

One of his followers, a Jewish man named Joseph of Arimathea, got permission from the Romans to take Jesus's body down from the cross. Joseph wrapped Jesus's body in a linen shroud and buried him inside a stone tomb he had bought for himself some years earlier. The promised Christ, Jesus come to save us, God right here among us, the eternal Son who is fully God and fully man—*dead*.

Death is the tragic part in most stories. The hero falls and the curtain drops. Some of the world's best literature has taught us to suspect that kind of doom. Herman Melville, the great American novelist, mastered the craft. We know Melville best for his novel *Moby Dick*, but he also wrote several short stories. One such story, the last one he ever wrote, is titled "Billy Budd, Sailor."

The story is about a young man named Billy who was forced to enlist in the British navy. Billy, unlike most sailors at that time, was considered a virtuous person. He was a really good guy, the kind of guy everyone likes. His character was so spotless that the story's narrator explains, "Billy in many respects was little more than a sort of upright barbarian, much such perhaps as Adam presumably might have been ere the urbane Serpent wriggled himself into his company."[1]

In other words, Billy was practically sinless. He was like Adam *before* the Fall. Melville makes him the obvious Christ-figure in the story, and like the real Christ, Billy ends up unfairly condemned to death for a crime he didn't commit. Although there are layers of complexity and brilliance in the story, it concludes with Billy's execution, in the tragic way we might expect from a writer who adored Shakespeare. Tragedy is the point. The good guy dies. Everyone is sad.

That is the way we are supposed to feel. That is what tragedies do. They remind us about the utter brokenness around us, about the absurdity, and then they're over.

The story of Jesus's death has this tragic element in it. The gospel writer Luke, more vividly than the others, emphasized the innocence of Jesus in the moments before he was slain. In his trial before Pontius Pilate, the Roman prefect over Judea, Jesus was repeatedly declared guiltless. Pilate said so at least four times:

- "I find no guilt in this man" (23:4).
- "I did not find this man guilty of any of your charges against him" (verse 14).
- "Look, nothing deserving death has been done by him" (verse 15).
- "I have found in him no guilt deserving death" (verse 22).

But despite his insistence, Pilate eventually caved to an angry mob and orchestrated the crucifixion of Jesus. The sound of Jesus's innocence resounds in our ears as we read of his being mocked and beaten, and then, in case we might forget, one of the two criminals crucified beside Jesus pointed it out again. The first criminal railed at Jesus until the second criminal spoke up: "We are receiving the due reward of our deeds; but this man has done nothing wrong" (verse 41).

Then one more time, to really drive home the importance of Jesus's innocence, one of the Roman soldiers overseeing the crucifixion declared, "Certainly this man was innocent!" (verse 47).

Innocent, the man now hanging dead on a cross. *He's innocent.* The good guy has died. That is the point. And like in so many other stories, everything about this looks tragic, except for one glaring difference: Jesus didn't stay dead.

Right There with Them

In this story, *this* true story, for *this* good guy, death doesn't have the last say. In fact, the Bible tells us that Jesus's death was actually the defeat of death itself. Death had consumed him. He was gone, ended, buried. *But then he conquered death.* Jesus was raised from the dead. He is alive, real, new.

The Resurrection changes everything. It's the greatest triumph in all of history. It's what sets the Christian story apart from every other. And it also can be the hardest part to believe. We're not accustomed to the laws of nature being bent, especially when they have a track record like death's. That's just not how things work, at least not according to our experience, not in our miracle-anemic age. But the story of Jesus demands that we believe the Resurrection. It is more central to what he did than anything else. More than the fact that he was a good man and a great teacher and that he died a sacrificial death, Jesus was physically raised from the dead in a body like ours but made new.

It happened on the Sunday morning after he died. Two women who followed Jesus, both named Mary, went to the tomb at dawn to bring fragrant spices. It was the sort of thing people did back then. But when the two women arrived at the tomb, they were met by an angel. The spices weren't needed after all. There would be no rotting corpse, not in the tomb where Jesus had been laid.

"He is not here," the angel reported, "for he has risen, as he said" (Matthew 28:6).

Then they ran, of course, with a mixture of fear and joy, to share the news with his disciples. Later in the week, Luke and John tell us, Jesus himself showed up to all of them. He walked into the room where the disciples were gathered, and he "stood among them." He was right there with them, shoulder to shoulder, face to face, and he looked at them and said, "Peace be with you" (Luke 24:36, NIV).

They had heard that voice before. They had seen this man. They had fed thousands with him. They were on the boat that time he calmed the storm. They remembered how he saved Peter from drowning. They all recalled how it felt when their knees hit the wooden deck that night, still exhausted from a long day, scared half to death because of the swirling winds, and they could still hear themselves saying to him, "Truly you are the Son of God" (Matthew 14:33).

They remembered all that, and they remembered Jesus dying; John had even watched him take his last breath. And now, there he was, right in front of them, looking at them, talking to them.

A short time later he even appeared to Thomas, who hadn't been there when Jesus visited the first time. Thomas had refused to believe Jesus was alive until he saw him in person. So Jesus came that second time to speak straight to him. "Put your finger here," Jesus said, "and see

my hands; and put out your hand, and place it in my side. Do not disbe-
lieve, but believe." And Thomas did, and he confessed, "My Lord and my
God!" (John 20:27–28). Jesus was alive. He had been raised from the
dead, physically raised, in a body like ours but made new.

Paul said in 1 Corinthians, in his concise explanation of the gospel,
that Jesus also "appeared to more than five hundred brothers at one time"
(15:6). The book of Acts, which tells the story of the early church and the
apostles' mission to spread the gospel, makes the Resurrection the dominating theme of everything said about Jesus.[2] The apostles were still talking about Jesus only because he had come back from the dead, and when
they talked about him, they stressed the fact that he had done so.

Listeners back then and listeners now are left to take it or leave it. We
either believe the testimony of the first messengers or we don't, but those
are the only options. There's no room for a kind of mystical, internalized
sense of a resurrection in the minds of his followers. Either Jesus was
raised—*is raised*—or he is dead. He is alive, or he is not.

Toward What It Means

There are good reasons to believe he is alive. In recent years, solid books
have been written to defend the Resurrection as historically valid as well as
to speak directly to the doubts of our age. If you were to read these books
and consider all the data accessible, you might be surprised by what you
find. There is much more evidence for the Resurrection than against it.
But rather than get into those details here, I simply want to highlight the
significance of the Resurrection. You might be thinking, *Why does it matter? What does it change?* Your capacity to accept the truth of Jesus's resurrection has no effect on its validity, but your grasp of its importance will at
least help you understand its unparalleled part in the Christian story.

And the first thing to say, maybe the most obvious, is that Jesus's resurrection from the dead is what allows his death to be effective in our lives.

If death had the last word, then we're left to scratch our heads about the whole propitiation part. It doesn't matter what he says his death accomplished; if he is still dead, then we have no reliable grounds to think that any of God's story is true. If Jesus is still in the grave, then all the significance drawn from his death is pathetic well-wishing, a bright ending that his followers forced upon a tragic event. If Jesus is still dead, his dying didn't do anything.

But, on the other hand, if Jesus is raised from the dead, then whatever he says his death accomplished is what it truly accomplished. If he is alive, he has the right to tell us what happened on the cross. And because he is alive, he now directs the purpose behind his dying. He gave his life to rescue his people from their sins, and now he is raised to see that purpose through.

The Resurrection is the event upon which this whole story stands or falls. That's what the apostle Paul said. He explained that if Jesus wasn't raised from the dead, whoever trusts in him is wasting his or her time (see 1 Corinthians 15:14). A dead savior is no savior.[3] That means the stakes are high, so high that the implications of the Resurrection are wondrously vast, even inexhaustible. In fact, we could say that the entire New Testament exists only because of the Resurrection and that its most basic purpose is to show us what the Resurrection means.

But of all the amazing implications of the Resurrection, there are three in particular that connect to our longing for significance and happiness. That is the state we are in, remember? All of us, created to enjoy and resemble and reflect the glory of God, have swapped that out for shallow thrills, and we're still looking, glory chasing and pleasure seeking, snubbing God and spreading lies. *Which is why Jesus came.* He lived as the true human we couldn't be, enjoying and resembling and reflecting God's glory for us. Then he died to absorb the punishment we deserved. And now he is raised. He is alive. *So why does that matter? What does that change?*

1. This Is Not Just a Story

The resurrection of Jesus takes the Christian story to a whole new level. This is still a story, a true story with ups and downs and an overall plot, but it isn't a mere story. It's not the kind of story that can be casually read by neutral bystanders. It's not the kind whose content can be dispassionately observed. If this is just a good story, simply a tale like all the others, then we can enjoy it for entertainment, pat it on the head, and get on with our lives.

But if it's more than a story, if it's actually a storied insight into the heart of unchangeable reality, then our very reading of the story gets swallowed up in the story itself. We realize we're not just being talked about; we're being *spoken to.*

Intrinsic to the Christian story is that its readers are part of it and that it demands a response. One theologian explained that the Bible functions as a kind of script that "calls not only for responsive reading but for responsive action and embodiment."[4] In other words, there are *things we must do* when it comes to *this story.* Nothing makes that clearer than Jesus's resurrection.

The early messengers of the gospel understood this. In the first sermon by an apostle in the book of Acts, Peter showed an unrelenting focus on the Resurrection. He put the resurrection of Jesus in the context of the ancient Jewish prophecies about the promised Christ, and he said boldly that Jesus was the One they'd been waiting for: "This Jesus God raised up, and of that we all are witnesses" (2:32).

Inseparable from Jesus's resurrection, Peter explained, was that Jesus is exalted. Jesus's identity as the Son of God is vindicated. Jesus is alive and reigning and is working through his Spirit to empower the telling and hearing of his story (see verses 32–35).

To wrap up the whole sermon, Peter ended with the obvious conclusion: "Let all the house of Israel therefore know for certain that God has made him both Lord and Christ, this Jesus whom you crucified" (verse 36). One paraphrase puts it, "There's no longer room for doubt—God made him Master and Messiah" (MSG).

The Resurrection has proved that Jesus is the promised Christ, the Savior come to save us, God right here among us, the eternal Son who is fully God and fully man.

Now the response of those first hearers to Peter makes perfect sense.

After those last words about who Jesus is, Luke tells us that the crowd was "cut to the heart" (verse 37). That is the literal expression in the original Greek. Conceptually, it means that things got real.

The deep rumblings of their souls, the complexities of their lives, all the things that swirled in the minds of people just trying to make it in this world—it all became exposed. Reality was felt as it is. The fluff was set aside. What really matters suddenly mattered to them, and they asked, "What shall we do?" (verse 37).

They knew this wasn't just a story. Something had to be different now. We see this again some years later when Paul preached in Antioch, an old metropolis located by the border of modern-day Turkey and Syria. In that sermon, after retracing key points in the Bible's story line, Paul claimed that the resurrection of Jesus guaranteed the fulfillment of God's promises. Like Peter, Paul connected the Resurrection to past prophecies about the promised Christ, and then he was clear about what it means for us: "Let it be known to you therefore, brothers, that through this man forgiveness of sins is proclaimed to you, and by him everyone who believes is freed from everything from which you could not be freed by the law of Moses" (Acts 13:38–39).

The story reaches the hearts of its hearers. The resurrection of Jesus means that we can be forgiven for our sins. Jesus is raised. His death matters. And therefore *you* can be forgiven. *You.*

We can't just passively listen to this. Here is where the Resurrection calls our bluff. Either we embrace this news and participate in its wonder, or we reject it and keep running down every dead-end road, down all those paths that have already been tried before.

Jesus gave his life as a sacrifice for your sins, and then he was raised from the dead. Jesus is alive, and forgiveness is proclaimed to you. This is freedom held out for you. Receive him, believe him, embrace him.

That is what an early messenger of the gospel would say to us all.

2. Our Response Is Personal

So the resurrection of Jesus means the Christian story is not just a story; it calls for our response. And because Jesus is raised, it also means our response is personal. It's *personal* as opposed to impersonal. It's *relational* instead of theoretical.

The apostle Paul called himself an ambassador for Christ. That's the way he described his work in 2 Corinthians: "We are ambassadors for Christ, God making his appeal through us. We implore you on behalf of Christ, be reconciled to God" (5:20).

Paul meant that he worked for Jesus. He implored listeners on Jesus's behalf. Behind everything he said about Jesus *was* Jesus himself, risen from the dead, alive, watching and working.[5] Paul's passionate appeals to people to believe in Jesus were an extension of Jesus's own appeals. And that means that how we respond to the message of Jesus is our response *to Jesus.*

Our response has a remarkably personal nature to it, and that begins to help us understand more of what that response should be.

The Christian story is ultimately about Jesus himself. It is news; it is an announcement (see 1 Corinthians 15:3–4), but it's never been flat content. At the center of it all is the declaration of a person—a person who has been raised from the dead, who has done real work in real history to reconcile real people to a real God.

Jesus stands over all gospel writers as the gospel Lord, and that means when people share his message, they're not passing along ideas; they're introducing *him*. They're introducing one person to another person. If gospel messengers were meant to merely blast out information, Jesus would have told his church to go make subscribers, not disciples (see Matthew 28:18–20). But because the Christian story is a message about Jesus, the real person, our response is not about what we do with the data but what we do with *him*.

And the call is to *believe* him.

The word for this in the original Greek is *pistis*, which we translate as "faith" (noun) and "believe" (verb). Paul spelled it out in his letter to the Galatians: "We know that a person is not justified by works of the law but through *faith in Jesus Christ*, so we also have *believed in Christ Jesus*, in order to be justified by *faith in Christ* and not by works of the law, because by works of the law no one will be justified" (2:16).

To be justified means to be made right with God. It means that God considers you righteous—as righteous as Jesus, the truest human to ever live. And Paul said we don't get there by our own working. There's nothing we can *do* to make it happen. Instead, we *believe* Jesus.

That's when the exchange happens: the wrath that stood against us for our unrighteous lives was taken away by Jesus on the cross; *it's gone*. And the righteousness of Jesus's life in his own enjoying and resembling and reflecting God's glory is given to us; *it's ours*. This is how we are declared right in God's sight. This is how we are reconciled to God (see 2 Corinthians 5:20): by believing Jesus.

And faith, our believing Jesus because he is a person, means more than acknowledging his existence. It means embracing him for who he is.

It's sort of like the difference between how we talk about others when they're not around versus how we talk about them when they're in the room.[6]

When the people who are the topic of conversation are not there, we tend to talk in broad judgments and mere statements. None of it has to be bad, but we just speak more in generalizations. We don't feel the pressure to be specific or to really agree or disagree.

But when these people are in the room, we talk and act differently. What we say is an actual affirmation or denial of them as they are, and they're standing right there beside us. We are more precise. We are careful to be accurate. We are talking on their terms, not ours.

Well, faith in Jesus is like that.

We're not able to stand at a distance and casually nod when statements are made about him. There are no generalizations here. The Resurrection means that when we hear the gospel we are put on the spot to embrace Jesus as he is, because he's standing in the room. He's right there beside us.

3. Faith Happens in the Heart

Jesus is raised from the dead, and therefore the Christian story is not just a story. It demands a response, and that response, because Jesus is raised and real, is personal—the gospel calls us to believe *him*.

But what exactly is faith? What does it mean to believe Jesus?

Because Jesus is a person, a real person who has been raised from the dead, he has intangible, aesthetic qualities that faith comprehends.

Even on the level of our common relationships, when we talk about putting our faith in someone, we mean that we deem the qualities of that person worthy of our trust. Trusting someone—*believing* that person—inevitably taps into our affections. This is why it hurts so much when the object of our trust doesn't pan out like we hoped. Relying upon someone involves the heart.

Two passages in the Bible stand out when it comes to faith in Jesus and to our affections. The first is from Paul in 2 Corinthians. In the context of describing his ministry, Paul mentioned the negative effect of his preaching. It wasn't always so cheery when he talked about Jesus. There were some folks who didn't get it. They might have heard what he said, but they were oblivious to its magnitude. He wrote, "In their case the god of this world has blinded the minds of the unbelievers, to keep them from seeing the light of the gospel of the glory of Christ, who is the image of God" (4:4).

In the eighteenth century, the American theologian Jonathan Edwards commented on this verse: "Nothing can be more evident, than that a saving belief of the gospel is here spoken of, by the apostle, as arising from the mind being enlightened to behold the divine glory of the things it exhibits."[7]

Translation: faith comes from seeing the worthiness of Jesus.

Paul said that those who *do not* believe the gospel *fail to see* Jesus for who he is. Edwards, therefore, inferred that those who *do* believe the gospel *must see* Jesus for who he is.

According to Paul, believing is "seeing the light of the gospel of the glory of Christ, who is the image of God" (2 Corinthians 4:4). Faith is *getting* the glory of Jesus. It's when it clicks. It's when people see his character and qualities and say, "Yes!"

Believing in Jesus is the affectional embrace of Jesus as worthy and glorious.[8]

Drinking It Up

The gospel of John also makes this point. The theme of faith is actually central to John's gospel, where "the verb *believe* occurs . . . over ninety times."[9] John even said his purpose in writing his account was "so that you may believe that Jesus is the Christ, the Son of God, and that by believing you may have life in his name" (20:31).

In 6:35, Jesus said, "I am the bread of life; whoever comes to me shall not hunger, and whoever believes in me shall never thirst."

Notice the parallel construction in this verse: *Coming* to Jesus is like *eating* (it means not being hungry). *Believing* in Jesus is like *drinking* (it means not being thirsty).

Jesus is the feast for our famished souls. He is the bottomless cup of cold water for our parched tongues. Believing in Jesus means that our deepest longings are satisfied.

All the glory chasing and pleasure seeking has blistered our hearts. It's as if we've been stuck in an avalanche of snow up to our waists on a cloudless day in January. We don't have any coats. Unbridled wind is chapping our faces. Our throats are frozen dry. Our stomachs are empty. Our toes are aching, whatever is left of them. As our heads are pounding in pain and our senses become even more disoriented, we don't think we're going to make it.

Then someone comes, almost out of nowhere, and digs us out of the snow, leads us to his cabin, seats us next to a crackling fire, throws a cozy blanket over us, and hands us a warm slice of buttered toast and a cup of hot coffee. When we finally hear his voice, it all makes sense. He tells us, "I am the blanket. I am the toast. I am the coffee. And you're never going to be cold or hungry or thirsty again."

So we stay there, and we eat and drink.

That is what it means to believe.

THE SEARCH IS OVER

When Jesus says we will never hunger or thirst again, he is saying that our search for significance and happiness is over. We can stop the chasing and seeking. We can stop our wanderings down all those other paths. We can stop looking elsewhere; in fact, we *must* stop looking elsewhere (the Bible calls this repentance). When we sit next to that fire and eat that toast and drink that coffee, we agree with him that there is no other fire or toast or coffee like this. So we're not going anywhere. We don't want to.

Jesus has come to save us, and he says he's exactly what we've been looking for, exactly what we need. And he can say that because he is raised from the dead. He is alive and real, standing in the room, right there beside us, *for us*.

And he even does more than that.

10

Hope Is Here

> You will not be happy if you are unable to
> possess what you love, be that what it may;
> nor can you be happy if you do not love what
> you have, be it ever so good; nor even if you
> are able to have what you love, if it be harmful
> to you.
>
> —Augustine

Peter had become an old man.

Thirty years had passed since he almost drowned that night, since that moment when Jesus gripped his arms in the raging winds and pulled him safely out of the sea.

Now, in this moment, all these years later, he gripped a pen with his wrinkled, calloused fingers and pulled out a piece of parchment. He remembered all he had seen and heard, and with a smile on his face, he penned the words "Blessed be the God and Father of our Lord Jesus Christ! According to his great mercy, he has caused us to be born again to a living hope through the resurrection of Jesus Christ from the dead" (1 Peter 1:3).

Peter was speaking to those who have believed in Jesus, both then and now. He was speaking to those who, like himself, have been surprised by Jesus and found in him what they've always longed for. And he said that Jesus's indestructible life has secured for us an inheritance that is "imperishable, undefiled, and unfading" (verse 4).

Jesus has led us into a whole new reality that cannot be corrupted, and he's given us a destiny far better than any we could ever imagine. In fact, it is this future destiny that makes the current reality what it is. The future is so glorious and so put together that it reaches back into today, to where we are now, and it breathes new life into how we see the world and ourselves. One theologian explained, "When faith is in fullest operation, it pictures a future with a God who is so powerful and so loving and so wise and so satisfying that this future-picturing faith experiences assurance. Now."[1] That is why Peter called it a "living hope."

The apostle Paul called it "the hope of the glory of God."

Paul said this in chapter 5 of his famous letter to the Romans. He began the discussion in the previous chapter by talking about faith, explaining that when we believe in Jesus we are justified, or declared right, in God's sight (see 4:22–24). He then went on to say, "Therefore, since we have been justified by faith, we have peace with God through our Lord Jesus Christ" (5:1).

This new relationship of peace with God is the new reality into which Jesus has led us. It's what Paul called "this grace in which we stand." And because of this reality, this grace through Jesus, we also have a new joy. Paul said, "Through [Jesus] we have also obtained access by faith into this grace in which we stand, and *we rejoice in hope of the glory of God*" (verse 2).

"We rejoice in hope of the glory of God." There it is.

The New Joy

Because of Jesus's death and resurrection for us, because of our faith in him, because of the new relationship with God that he has led us into, we who have fallen short of God's glory can now rejoice in hope of it.

Sin has meant that we lack the glory of God (see Romans 3:23).

But sin forgiven, wrath removed, peace with God, faith in Jesus because of what he has done—that means the glory of God will be ours.

It means that, through Jesus, God's glory is ours now, and it will be more fully ours in a deeper, uninhibited way found only in the world to come. The enchanted beginning of our story, the place we've fallen from, is now that to which we are restored, *and beyond*.

This is the path we're on, and it's our story from here on out.

This is our hope, our "living hope," and it is the foundation of our happiness. It makes us rejoice now and anticipate even more rejoicing because we know there's more to come. Paul said it this way: this hope "does not put us to shame" (Romans 5:5). The hope won't disappoint. It's absolutely guaranteed.

But how do we know that?

How can we be so sure that this hope won't put us to shame? How do we know that we've found the significance we've been longing for, that there is more of it waiting for us, and that it will be all it's cracked up to be?

The Holy Spirit is how.

Again, in Paul's words: "And hope does not put us to shame, because God's love has been poured into our hearts through the Holy Spirit who has been given to us" (5:5).

God has done something amazing. He has poured his love into our hearts by giving us his Holy Spirit.

That is the reason our hope in God's glory is certain. Our hope won't put us to shame *because we have the Spirit.* The Spirit, then, is the guarantee that we will find in God all that we've ever wanted and all that we could ever need.[2]

The relationship between the Spirit and our hope is important and pervasive in the New Testament. The salvation that Jesus has accomplished for us has an unmistakable future aspect to it; we are changed now, and, yes, there is an even better future ahead. And it is the Spirit who helps us get there. He is the One with us in *this* world to keep our eyes on the *next.* There's more to say about this in the next chapter, but let's begin by looking at who the Spirit is and what he does in our lives.

THE SPIRIT FROM FOREVER

You have probably heard something about the Holy Spirit before, and whatever that might be, the Spirit is still more important than we often think.[3] The Christian story simply doesn't make sense until we understand him, and we could never journey down this path without his power.

For us to understand who the Spirit is, it helps to remember that the Spirit, like Jesus, didn't just pop into existence when he stepped onto the stage of the New Testament. The Spirit has been at work in the world since its creation,[4] and he is as eternal as the Father and the Son.

We saw in chapter 2 that before there was even a universe there was God, and he was (as he is) a God of love. Essentially, in himself, from forever, God is the Father loving the Son in the unceasing fellowship of the Holy Spirit. And that should lead us to wonder, *If the Spirit has always been there with the Father and Son, what is he doing? What is his role within the Trinity?*

The Bible doesn't say straightforwardly, "Hey, this is what the Spirit has been doing from forever," but it does say enough about the Spirit that we can put some pieces together. That's what Jonathan Edwards did a few hundred years ago in an essay he wrote on the Trinity. He explained that the Spirit is the "holy and sacred energy" that exists between the Father and Son. The Spirit is the mutual love and delight that the Father and Son have always experienced for each other in their fellowship.[5]

When we think about the Spirit within the Trinity, we should think of him as we normally would think of a spirit, as a kind of invisible force or energy. The biblical words for the Spirit, *ruach* in Hebrew and *pneuma* in Greek, actually mean "wind" or "breath."[6] And within the Trinity, this force-energy-wind-breath is the person of the Holy Spirit who personifies the divine love and delight. The Holy Spirit is the divine love and delight *breathed out*.[7]

That is why Paul could say that *God's love in us* is *the Spirit given to us* (see Romans 5:5). The Spirit who has eternally lived as the personal energy of the loving fellowship between the Father and the Son is the Spirit who is now given to those who believe. If you're like me, this probably makes your head spin. If it does, that's okay; just start back from the top and read it again slowly. That's what I did. We're talking about deep things here, but remember, our souls are asking deep questions.

HEY, YOU KNOW HIM

In the gospel of John we read that on the night before his crucifixion, sitting around a table with his disciples, Jesus taught them more about the Holy Spirit.

He knew that he would die soon and that the disciples would be left in confusion. Even in that moment, sitting around the table, he knew that their hearts were already troubled. So he spoke to encourage them. He looked to a time after his death, after his resurrection, after he ascended to take his seat on his heavenly throne,[8] and he told them, "I will ask the Father, and he will give you another advocate to help you and be with you forever—the Spirit of truth. The world cannot accept him, because it neither sees him nor knows him. But you know him, for he lives with you and will be in you" (John 14:16–17, NIV).

It's hard to say what you would have done if you had been sitting there with the disciples when Jesus said this. They were still learning who *he* was and what *he* meant,[9] and now, hours before his gruesome death, he was saying good-bye and briefing them about a Spirit who would come after he was gone.

If I had been there, my face would have looked more puzzled than I imagine the disciples' faces were. If there was ever a time to doubt—and there were many such times—this had to be the foremost. What in the world would Jesus say to defuse their confusion?

"You know him," Jesus said, "for he lives with you and will be in you" (verse 17, NIV).

Jesus explained that the coming of the Spirit—this Advocate, the One he'd send—meant the disciples would not be alone. It meant that although Jesus would not be there in person, he'd still be there, still be *here*.

This was the way Jesus chose to encourage his closest friends, and there was nothing sentimental about it. He did not mean that he'd still be around in their memories. He wasn't comforting this group of men with the same kind of platitudes whispered to people at modern funerals. Jesus meant that he was really going to be there.

His Spirit, the One he'd known from forever, the personal force of love between him and the Father, the personal energy who indwelled and empowered his life on earth, was coming to live inside his followers.

Jesus had come to earth as *God with us, right here among us.*

The Spirit would come, Jesus said, as *God in us, right here inside us.*

As if God coming to us as a human like us wasn't impressive enough, as if dying on a cross for us didn't push things over the edge, *now God was moving to live within us.* He was coming to live in the hearts of people like you and me, hearts as filthy as the stable where Jesus first cried and as dark as the cross where Jesus last cried. We have these dusty, black hearts, and Jesus said the Spirit will make them his home.

I can hear the thoughts running through your head: *Is this some kind of joke? Was Jesus being serious?*

Yeah, he was serious.

And the Spirit did come.

After Jesus was raised from the dead, just before he ascended, he instructed his disciples to wait together in Jerusalem for his Spirit to descend on them. Luke the historian said it happened on the day of Pentecost, as they were all together at a friend's house, waiting just as Jesus had told them to: "Suddenly there came from heaven a sound like a mighty rushing wind" (Acts 2:2)—like a wind, like how we'd expect a spirit to come—and the Spirit filled the disciples.

The Spirit was poured into them, given to them, and they were never the same.

THE SAME SPIRIT

The disciples were never the same because one of the things they most loved about Jesus had become part of them. The life that emanated from his words, the energy of his presence—*that* life and energy took up residence within their souls, in their own words, their own presence. They were still men, dirty elbows and lunch on their faces, but now they were *anointed* men. They were men filled with the Spirit, which Jesus had said was a lot like being filled with himself.

Back before he died, sitting around that same table on that same night, that's pretty much what he told his disciples. Jesus said to them, "In that day [when the Spirit comes] you will know that I am in my Father, and you in me, *and I in you*" (John 14:20).

Jesus said this again in his final prayer for the disciples and for everyone who believes in him. Speaking to the Father, he prayed, "I made known to them your name, and I will continue to make it known, that the love with which you have loved me may be in them, *and I in them*" (17:26).

In other words, Jesus prayed, "Put that same love in them—the Spirit, who is like me."[10]

The apostles talked the same way. Sometimes they even said straight up that Jesus is in believers, by which they meant the Spirit is in believers—the same Spirit who was in Jesus, who is a lot like Jesus.

John even assured us, "And by this we know that [Jesus] abides in us, by the Spirit whom he has given us" (1 John 3:24). He meant that Jesus is in us by his Spirit in us.

In Romans, Paul wrote, "Anyone who does not *have the Spirit of Christ* does not belong to him. But if Christ *is in you,* although the body is dead because of sin, the Spirit is life because of righteousness" (8:9–10).

So track with him: having the Spirit is described in the first sentence as Christ being in you in the sentence after it. The phrases are basically interchangeable. "Christ in you" means "his Spirit in you." When Paul said that Jesus "lives in me," he meant that the Spirit lived in him (Galatians 2:20).

The same Spirit who indwelled Jesus, who has been the personal force of love between him and the Father from forever, lives inside all who believe. And when that Spirit, that personal energy, is in us, it's like Jesus is in us.

While Old Testament promises spoke about God's Spirit being poured out among his people, the disciples had not connected the dots, at least not yet. The same Spirit who indwelled the Messiah would also indwell the individual hearts of those who believed in him. *This was new,* and it was turning the world upside down in all the right kind of ways.

Paul actually said this in the first chapter of his letter to the Colossians. He started by journaling about the gospel's advance and describing the scope of his ministry. He reported that all the nations were hearing the good news of Jesus and discovering the amazing mystery of God's salvation.

People like you and me, Paul said, were being blown away by the wonder of what God was doing in the world. And Paul summarized that wonder as "Christ in you, the hope of glory" (verse 27).

Peter called it a living hope. Paul said it was the hope of glory.

And the amazing truth of it all is that it's a hope for here.

11

Born All Over Again

Now the whole offer which Christianity makes
is this: that we can, if we let God have His
way, come to share in the life of Christ. . . .
The whole purpose of becoming a Christian is
simply nothing else.

—C. S. Lewis

W e have hope because of the Holy Spirit, because he connects us
to Jesus.

The Spirit is the One who swallows up our little lives into the grand
story of God's salvation by swallowing up our lives into Jesus himself.
The Spirit joins us to Jesus in an unbreakable bond. As the Spirit has been
the eternal, personal energy of fellowship between the Father and Jesus,
the Spirit becomes, in a similar way, the energy between Jesus and all who
believe in him.

This truth has historically been called "union with Christ," and it
really is the description of God's salvation in the New Testament.[1] It's sort
of like the go-to expression to describe what Jesus has accomplished in the
lives of those who trust him.

To be *saved by Jesus* is to be *united to Jesus*.

To put your faith in Jesus is, as Paul said, to be found in Christ (see Philippians 3:8–9).

All the good effects of Jesus's life, death, and resurrection become ours *because the Spirit joins us to him*—and joins us to him such that his life becomes ours, his death ours, his resurrection ours. What Jesus did counts for us as if we did it too.

This means that our being forgiven, justified, and reconciled to God comes to us as gifts found in our solidarity with Jesus. We don't receive anything from him that comes apart from him. Everything that our souls most want and need is found *in Jesus* and only in Jesus. And we get him and his gifts only by the Spirit who connects us to him.

YOUR NEW IDENTITY

Now, a couple of chapters ago, you might recall, I said that the gifts of forgiveness and reconciliation are made ours *through faith*. Paul tells us we are justified *through faith* in Jesus Christ (see Galatians 2:16). We experience Jesus's salvation *when we see* him for who he is, *when we understand* his worthiness, *when we taste* the buttered toast and hot coffee he is for our frigid souls.

All that is true, which might make you wonder, *Does our salvation come through faith or through the Spirit? Which is it?*

It's both because it's the Spirit who makes us *see* and *understand* and *taste*. The Spirit is the One who authors our faith.

We'd still be buried in the avalanche if it wasn't for him. We'd still be out there, still alone, still dying. But when the Spirit moves, like a gust of wind, Jesus said, he opens our eyes and thaws our senses. To believe in Jesus is to embrace Jesus, and the Spirit is the One who orchestrates and empowers that embrace. He's the One who throws that blanket over us and brings us into the cabin. He's the One who hands us the buttered toast and coffee and makes us able to hear Jesus's voice. The Spirit is the One who unites us to Jesus our Savior and irreversibly redefines who we are. He marks the end of who we used to be—stuck within our fallen humanity—and he gives us a whole new identity.

It's an identity so new and different that the biblical imagery describes it as being born all over again.[2] Think about that for a minute. This is supposed to be as new as you could possibly get. You may have heard the phrase *born-again Christian* before. Well, this is where it comes from.

We were first born into the system of Adam. We were part of the fallen humanity where we snubbed God, swapped his glory for trifles, and ran hard down every dead-end road. But now, in Jesus, because the Spirit has swept us up into his death and resurrection, we are born again into a new way of life: no longer in Adam, *but now in Jesus.* We are "born again to a living hope" (1 Peter 1:3). "If anyone is in Christ," Paul wrote, "he is a new creation. The old has passed away; behold, the new has come" (2 Corinthians 5:17).

And this is it. This new reality into which the Spirit has brought us, our new identity found in our union with Jesus, is what we've been looking for this whole time. This is where we discover the significance and happiness we've been craving.

THEN AND NOW

We are all glory chasers and pleasure seekers, remember. We all want to be connected to something big and wonderful, and we all want to have joy. We all have a hunger for glory and gladness. And that's because God made us for those things. He made us to resemble and reflect *his* glory, to find our greatness in *his* greatness, and to live in the pleasure that is *his* fellowship.

This is why nothing else will do. Nothing else will add up. No matter how far we get or how high we climb, something will always be missing unless we tap into that original glory and gladness at the heart of our existence.

And that is what Jesus *is*.

Jesus is that original glory. He is the fullness of joy. He is the One who perfectly resembled and reflected the glory of God *as* the glory of God embodied as a human like us. Jesus became like us in order to do what we couldn't, and to do it *for us*. And when we are united to him by the Spirit, we share with him in what's he done. We share in his significance and happiness; we are partakers of his glory;[3] and we do it all with our eyes set on the future he has planned for us.

That future is when we ourselves will be "glorified" (Romans 8:30). That's the Bible's word for when we will be dramatically transformed into the image of Jesus. It's when we'll perfectly look like the One who perfectly resembles and reflects the glory of God. John said in one of his letters that we don't know exactly what that'll be like, but we do know this: when Jesus appears at the Second Coming, "we shall be like him, because we shall see him as he is" (1 John 3:2).

Remember Paul said, "We rejoice in hope of the glory of God" (Romans 5:2).

Or as Peter told us, "Set your hope fully on the grace that will be brought to you at the revelation of Jesus Christ" (1 Peter 1:13).

Don't miss this. He said there's grace that will be brought to us and we should set our hope on that. There is more to this salvation that will be revealed to us "in the last time" (verse 5). He was talking about the glory yet to come, when we'll look just like Jesus, when we'll be changed, transformed, renewed. And it'll be so wondrous that it can't even be compared to anything we experience now (see Romans 8:18; 2 Corinthians 4:17).

As I mentioned in the last chapter, there is an unmistakable future aspect to what Jesus has accomplished for us. There is more to look forward to, and it's the Holy Spirit who keeps our heads up and eyes open. That's his ministry in our lives. He's the One who helps us look *there* from *here.* He fills us and fuels us to wait eagerly for that fuller glory that's just a little way out (see Romans 8:23; Galatians 5:5). Paul even called the Spirit the down payment for what's to come (see 2 Corinthians 1:22; Ephesians 1:14, csb). That means the Spirit is the present experience of a greater, future reality. He's the proof that there is a future, and he lets us in on that *now.*

The Holy Spirit, because he unites us to Jesus and assures us of hope, is the only way to true significance and happiness in this life.

The Happiness Criteria

According to Augustine, the basic criteria for happiness is first, that we have what we love; second, that we love what we have; and third, that it not be a bad thing (or in other words, we must love an object worthy of love).[4]

Augustine's point is pretty much true all across the spectrum, even for little things. He's basically laid out the simplest ingredients for contentment. It's the explanation for why I'm happy drinking coffee and watching the Saint Louis Cardinals win baseball games. Possessing the things we love, when they're decent things, produces happiness.

But if this is true of little things, what about for bigger things? How would this play out for the greatest of all loves? How does this work with God?

Well, God is the supreme good. He is the most lovable object in the universe, and he has given himself to us in his Son.

Jesus shows us God's nature, and he brings us into relationship with

God through his death and resurrection. So for humans to really be happy, we must love and possess *Jesus*. We must be united to him, sharing in how he perfectly resembles and reflects God's glory, and sharing in the joy of that divine fellowship. That is true happiness.

And there's more.

Augustine wrote, "The happiness which an intelligent being desires as its legitimate object is the reality of the combination of two things: namely, that it enjoy the Immutable Good, which is God, *without interruption;* and that it know with a certainty that it is exempt alike from doubt as from error, *that it shall abide in that enjoyment forever.*"[5]

Translation: the happiness we humans desire—the happiness for which we were made—requires our possession of God to be unhindered and irrevocable.

We have to experience Jesus in the fullest way and with undoubtable permanence.

When we talk about a relationship like that, we're talking about the future. That kind of relationship with Jesus, that kind of divine fellowship, is what heaven is going to be.

And the Holy Spirit comes in because he's meant to be that heaven here on this earth. He's our down payment. He's the assurance *now* of that unhindered, irrevocable possession that is *yet to come* (see Ephesians 1:14).

The true, eternal happiness we crave is out of this world, literally. The only way we can experience any piece of it in this world is by the Holy Spirit, and the Spirit is that for us because he unites us to Jesus.

THE JOY OF ANOTHER WORLD

This union with Jesus really is the joy of another world. It's like something we're used to, but then not used to at all. It's like the pleasure of coming home, of breathing in deeply the familiar aromas of the place we love, but we didn't know they were familiar until the moment we breathed them in. And in that moment, when the scent overwhelms our senses, it feels like Christmas morning times a thousand.

This is the pleasure of being united to the One who created pleasure itself, the One who is himself eternal pleasure and joy, and from whom every other good thing is but a momentary sparkle.[6]

This is the pleasure that takes its cues not in circumstances but in that timeless, imperturbable reality of hope in God, of what God has told us will be. For now, we suffer. We bear a cross. We are grieved by various trials. Sometimes we cry day and night. If we're looking for significance in the stuff around us, in something like our performance, then it's only as good as we can keep up. If we're looking for happiness in how today goes, then it's only as reliable as the tread on our tires.

The true significance and happiness we crave is found only in Jesus.

"And after you have suffered a little while," Peter tells us, "the God of all grace, who has called you to his eternal glory in Christ, will himself restore, confirm, strengthen, and establish you" (1 Peter 5:10). We experience something here, but we don't get it all. Not now. But it is still *something*.

That all makes it difficult to describe.

Old Peter, wrinkled, calloused fingers gripping the pen, with a smile on his face, said it like this in his first letter: "Though you have not seen him, you love him. Though you do not now see him, you believe in him and rejoice with joy that is inexpressible and filled with glory" (1:8).

He called it "inexpressible joy," maybe not just because it's too good to put into words but maybe because it's too difficult. It's as though he were saying, "How can I tell you what this is like?"

We can try, but we don't know. We're attempting to express what the apostle calls "inexpressible."

It *is* happiness, though; that is sure. And it's filled with significance. It's a happiness of meaning, a deep joy that flows from what's big and great and matters most.

And there will be more of it to come.

For now we have the Spirit, and we have hope. We have the wonder of our union with Jesus and the fact that we've found what we've been looking for. We've discovered the significance and happiness we've craved, and it makes us feel like we belong. It makes us feel like we're doing what we should do, like we're more human than we've ever been before. Though we've abandoned so much of who we used to be in our fallen humanity, we've uncovered, without even meaning to, our truest selves. And whatever it is we learn to say about it, we know that, at the very least, it's not stupid normal.

The Path Together

So you're a glory chaser and pleasure seeker. All of us are. And we're this because God made us to be this. It's the wonder of being human. The problem is that sin, like an angry hand with sharp nails, has dug its hold into the chalkboard of this wonder and screeched a claw mark from one end to the other. The mark has stretched all the way through, and while the soul of every human bristles, we're mostly just confused . . . and still hungry.

We still want significance and happiness, but we're stuck searching in all the wrong places, all of us running down all the same dead-end roads, because the only comfort in being lost is the illusion that we're not lost alone. But we are. We, in our brokenness and sin, rebel against God, lust after autonomy, and hoist up trifles—until God himself comes to save us.

That's what Jesus did.

He came and lived and died and was raised to bring us back into fellowship with God, to reunite us with the significance and happiness for which we were made. And Jesus does this by uniting us to *himself* by the power of his Spirit. His Spirit in us is the assurance that one day our glory and joy will be unhindered and irrevocable. We experience it now in part—not less than what it is, just not as fully as it will be. And it *will be,* one day. That's where this path is leading, more sure than the sun that rises.

But for now, here's the thing: Knowing that our fellowship with Jesus is real, how do we experience more of it? The significance and happiness found in Jesus is indeed that, *significance and happiness,* but how do we get more of him in our lives?

MORE OF THE TRUER AND BETTER

A couple of friends of mine, fellow pastors at Cities Church in Minneapolis, have written some helpful books on this topic. One book is about practical habits we can develop, called *Habits of Grace,*[1] and the other book is about the way we should see the stuff of this world, called *The Things of Earth.*[2] Both books are about getting more of Jesus, and I happily, wholeheartedly recommend them.

But if I could mention only two things at the close of a short book, two means through which we experience more of Jesus in our lives and more of the significance and happiness found in him, they are, in a word each, *community* and *obedience.*

By *community,* I'm referring to the local church; and by *obedience,* I'm referring to doing what Jesus says. These means are different, but they're not disconnected, and the first is foundational.

GOD'S PLAN FROM THE START

The local church is one of the most important things that any of us could be part of. If you are a follower of Jesus and you've been flying solo (or even if you're just interested in Jesus and you've been considering pursuing him alone), then getting plugged into a local community of Christians should be top priority. This has to do with what the church is by her very nature.

From the beginning, God's plan to rescue humanity was a plan to rescue *a people*. This might require a paradigm shift in your thinking, but basically, to be saved by God is to be saved into the people of God, into something bigger than yourself. We can see the start of this even in the Garden of Eden.

Adam and Eve, created in the image and likeness of God, created to enjoy, resemble, and reflect the glory of God, were given a commission: "Be fruitful and multiply and fill the earth" (Genesis 1:28). This commission is another way of God saying "Advance what you have here. Take this and extend it. Reproduce it!"

And so we ask, "What if Adam and Eve had actually done that?"

If Adam and Eve, enjoying, resembling, and reflecting the glory of God, had been fruitful and multiplied and filled the earth, untarnished by sin, then it would have meant a whole world inhabited by God's image-bearers who enjoy, resemble, and reflect his glory. It would have been a world full of worship, a whole world filled with people united as a people *by* and *in* and *for* God.

The plan was basically the vision God himself describes in Numbers 14:21: "All the earth shall be filled with the glory of the LORD."

That was God's plan way back in Genesis, and it's still God's plan today. Sin has never changed what he set out to do. When the march of God's redemption was launched, it wasn't about saving some individuals scattered here and there throughout history; it was about saving an entire people to call his own.

So there would be a Son born of a woman, born in a family, born in a nation, who would be the Savior of all the nations of the earth, forming with them an entirely new "nation" in itself (1 Peter 2:9). This is a promise first made to Adam and Eve, then to Abraham, and then passed down by generations; the promise of this Son, this Savior, this King continued all the way to the New Testament.

THE SHOCKING TRUTH

God is used to shocking the world. He never interacts with humanity in ways we'd expect, and *the church* definitely wasn't on anyone's radar. There was certainly a category for God saving a people. God shows us this salvation over and over again in the Old Testament in his faithfulness to Israel, in his plague-declaring, sea-parting, sin-forgiving, war-winning, prophet-sending, promise-making faithfulness to Israel. But it's the New Testament that finally tells us who this rescued people will ultimately be, and it's not merely Israel.

The people of God is actually a people of *peoples,* individuals from every tribe and language on this earth who become one people by their union to Jesus. It means Jews *and* Gentiles. It means Greeks *and* barbarians. It means anyone, regardless of his or her ethnicity, social status, or past; we're talking about a people consisting of anyone and everyone who trusts in Jesus and finds in him the significance and happiness we all crave.

Jesus creates this people, this *one, new people,* by demolishing all the invisible barriers that keep us apart. Paul calls these barriers the "the dividing wall of hostility" (Ephesians 2:14). Jesus, by his death, destroyed this wall to create a whole new humanity, one whose identity is so powerful that it transcends all the corporate identities that used to define us, even family.

Now, this doesn't mean that family doesn't matter, just that there is a bond that runs deeper than shared genes. Jesus told us this in the gospel of Mark. It was early in his teaching ministry, just early enough that people were still caught off guard by the unusual things he said. I can hear them asking, "What box do we put Jesus in? Who is this guy?"

His own family wondered that as much as anyone.

In Mark 3, Jesus was inside a home, teaching a crowd of followers sitting around him. Outside the doors, as Jesus was teaching, his mother and brothers came and presumably poked their heads in to get his attention. This had to be awkward. Mark tells us that someone in the crowd finally spoke up: "Your mother and your brothers are outside, seeking you" (verse 32).

Jesus replied, "'Who are my mother and my brothers?' And looking about at those who sat around him, he said, 'Here are my mother and my brothers! For whoever does the will of God, he is my brother and sister and mother'" (verses 33–35).

Jesus said something similar in the gospel of Luke. Again, as he was teaching, someone mentioned his family. A woman spoke up in the crowd around him and said, in vintage first-century fashion, "Blessed is the womb that bore you, and the breasts at which you nursed!" (11:27). In other words, this woman, likely a mom herself, told Jesus that his mom must sure be proud. This woman was amazed by Jesus's teaching, and she figured Mary was lucky to have him as a son. Jesus didn't say whether Mary was lucky or not. He just replied, "Blessed rather are those who hear the word of God and keep it!" (verse 28).

We can hardly appreciate the magnitude of those words.

Family is a big deal for a lot of people in our modern world, but it doesn't come close to the centrality that family held in ancient times. And right there, right in the middle of that world, right in the thick of that value system, Jesus said there is something more important than family. A blessing greater than genetic connections, a blessing greater than even a maternal bond, is the one shared by those who follow Jesus.

Going Local

There is a people who do God's will, a people who receive and embrace God's words. This is the people Jesus came to make. This is the church. Or as Paul said, "the household of God" (Ephesians 2:19; 1 Timothy 3:15).

We're not just talking about a new people but also a new family. And that family reality is felt most vividly in the church's local manifestations.

Two categories come into play when we talk about the church. First, there is the church *universal,* which refers to all Christians from all places over all time. This is the cross denominational, transhistorical communion shared by all those who believe the gospel. This is what is meant in the Apostles' Creed when we say, "We believe in the holy catholic church, the communion of saints." In this sense we're talking broadly about every true follower of Jesus.

Second, there is the church *local,* which refers to the smaller manifestations of the church that exist in specific times and settings. This is where we really begin to find that family feel. This is where we meet real flesh-and-blood people who are supposed to be for us our mother and sisters and brothers.

I realize this might still sound odd to you unless you've experienced it, because it is much better experienced than explained. My wife and I came to understand this firsthand when we moved from Raleigh to Minneapolis several years ago.

Right after college, still new to marriage and brand-new to parenting, we left all the family and friends we'd ever known to settle in a place where we didn't know anyone. The only connection we had was the local church we planned to join. We knew we'd find others there who did "the will of God," and so we clung to the words of Jesus in Mark 3. We have an amazing extended family and tons of support back in the Carolinas where we grew up, but moving so far away, we needed God to provide us new relationships on the ground. We needed the church to be our family the way Jesus said it would be. And that's what happened.

It didn't happen overnight, and it was never easy as pie, but the local church welcomed us. By investing in one place and committing to one people, within a year's time it was hard for us to imagine leaving. So we didn't leave. We ended up calling the Twin Cities home and were eventually commissioned to plant a daughter church within the metro area.

Honestly, I can't begin to tell you the impact the local church has had in my life and in my family. And it's not just the relationships themselves. This is not just about a group of people becoming friends. I'm talking about a community of Christians who have each experienced the power of the gospel in their lives and who therefore center their lives on that gospel together. I'm talking about individuals who have found in Jesus their true significance and happiness, who *want* more of him, and who *experience* more of him in this beautiful mutuality where the one is for the all and the all is for one another.

I think this is what Paul was getting at when he talked about the church growing up together and building itself up in love (see Ephesians 4:15–16). In this context, all the other means of grace are at work and flourishing. Habits like reading and studying the Bible, prayer, acts of service, corporate worship, and the Lord's table—all of these are made richer when they are part of a shared identity within the local church.

Remember, God didn't just save you, but he saved you into a people.

DOING WHAT JESUS SAYS

So when it comes to experiencing more of Jesus in our lives, and more of the significance and happiness found in him, there is *community,* by which I mean the local church. And then there is *obedience,* by which I mean doing what Jesus says. This is one of the most basic realities when it comes to following Jesus.

At the end of the gospel of Matthew, just before Jesus ascended, he commissioned his disciples: "Go therefore and make disciples of all nations, baptizing them in the name of the Father and of the Son and of the Holy Spirit, teaching them to observe all that I have commanded you" (28:19–20).

Straightforward here: to be a disciple of Jesus, a follower of Jesus, means we learn to observe all that he has commanded us. And when Jesus said *all* that he had commanded us, he wasn't just talking about his statements quoted in the four Gospels.

The "all that I have commanded you" extends beyond his recorded lines to include all the Spirit-inspired words of the entire New Testament. As Peter put it, "For no prophecy was ever produced by the will of man, *but men spoke from God as they were carried along by the Holy Spirit*" (2 Peter 1:21). In this sense, then, the entire New Testament is what Jesus was saying. To observe all that he has commanded us is to observe the whole thing.

So by obedience, by doing what Jesus said, I mean listening to the Bible. Obedience means conforming our lives to the revealed will of God in Scripture.

WHATEVER HE WANTS

This doesn't mean we have the exact answer for every single circumstance. The Bible is not a manual in that way. So much of life must be played out with gospel prudence. We take what the Bible tells us and we try our best, with the Spirit's help and in community, to apply its truth to all kinds of different situations. It will always start in our hearts before it gets expressed by our hands, and the main thing to nail down is simply that *we want whatever he wants.*

This, of course, makes sense. If we're united to Jesus, if we find in him our true significance and happiness, then absolutely we will want our own desires to line up with his. It was no accident that Jesus taught his disciples to pray, as the foundation, "Our Father in heaven, hallowed be your name. *Your kingdom come, your will be done*" (Matthew 6:9–10). When we experience fellowship with God, we will desire more of God— more of God in our own lives and more of God for others in this world.

That is what obedience is about.

But it's not always easy.

Sometimes, in fact, it's just plain hard. Sometimes obedience can feel like we're being yanked into the raging sea of uncertainty or the dark forest of suffering. Every time, though, obedience will ask more of us than what we are in ourselves. And that's the whole point.

JESUS IS REAL

One of the things that we say over and over again at Cities Church is that Jesus is real.

I'm convinced that one of our greatest needs is to awaken to the simple fact of his realness, that he's not just some historical figure or some character on a page. Jesus Christ is a *real person,* more real and more alive in this exact moment than any of us. If we only knew how real he is!

The problem, though, at least for the church in America, is not so much that we don't believe Jesus is real but that we've created a brand of Christianity where he doesn't need to be real. We're surrounded by a society that pretends Jesus is a myth, where the normal snapshot of reality excludes him. We have, too many times and in too many ways, adapted our faith to settle for this. We have bleached obedience of its demand that Jesus be who he says he is.

In other words, if obedience is not asking more of us than we are, then it won't lead us to more of Jesus. Obedience that doesn't need him won't have him. But really, there's no such thing as obedience like that.

The obedience we're called to—doing what Jesus says, conforming our lives to the will of God—can't happen apart from him. Even if it feels small, even if it seems easy, we will never want what he wants if not for his power in us. "No one can say 'Jesus is Lord' except in the Holy Spirit" (1 Corinthians 12:3). He will call us to live in a way that requires his presence and all his promises to be true, and we wouldn't want it any other way.

Earlier I mentioned that community and obedience share an important connection, and that might make more sense now. The best way to live in the obedience we're called to is when we're surrounded by, and locking arms with, those who get it. We learn to trust and obey Jesus more when we're doing life with others who believe Jesus is worthy of trust and obedience.

There, in a community like that, on the path of obedience together, we will get more of him. And the more of Jesus we experience, the more we will experience the significance and happiness for which we were made.

Study Guide

Chapter 1: The Stupid Normal

1. When in your life have you felt that there must be more to life than what you experience? What kind of effect does that thought have on you?

2. Have we really let the Self take the place of God? What are some examples of ways that we as a society have elevated the Self to possess unprecedented authority?

3. In your words, what is the American Dream? Why do you think people surrounded by this kind of prosperity still tend toward a "strange melancholy," as Alexis de Tocqueville once called the sadness he observed in America?[1]

4. What might *Nacho Libre* teach us about the cravings of the human heart? In your words, what does it mean to long for glory? What does that have to do with happiness?

5. How do you think about the intersection of our desire to have significance *and* happiness? Do you care about one more than the other?

Chapter 2: When You Think About God

1. What do you commonly think about when you think about God? What is the first thought that rises from your heart? Has it always been this way for you?

2. Have you ever considered how much your view of God affects the way you live? What are some examples of how someone's understanding of God influences his or her actions?

3. You may have heard this said before, but it seems like many atheists tend to be mad at the god they believe doesn't exist. Why do you think that is? Do you think that there is often more going on with people's intellectual objections to God?

4. If we humans could invent our own god, what might that god be like? What things would our god affirm and denounce?

5. *Exclusive humanism* is a fancy name for our culture's desire to be orphans. What are some of the symptoms of this desire? What are some of its overall effects?

Chapter 3: The Happy Father Who Loves

1. There are two categories for how we think about God: one category has to do with God in relation to other things; the second category has to do with God in his essence. What is an example of this latter category? Name one description of God in his essence, and explain.

2. The apostle John wrote, "God is love" (1 John 4:8). That is a simple and amazingly profound description of God. In what ways is it profound? What makes God's love a reality deeper than the universe?

3. How is God different from the way Oz, "the great and powerful," is depicted in *The Wizard of Oz*?

4. God is love, and God is happy. On what basis do we know that God is happy? How might this truth alone change the way you think about him?

5. What is one phrase that sums up the picture of God revealed in the Bible? If this picture were to become the default way you think about God, what kind of effect do you think it would have on your life?

Chapter 4: Starting with a Search

1. The human experience is full of both dignity and darkness. What are some examples of the two? What are evidences of human awesomeness, and what are evidences that something is broken?

2. What is *expressive individualism*? What are some ways you've seen this at work in our society? Where does it show up in popular culture?

3. Does the hunger for significance resonate with you? Have there been instances in your own life when you felt an absence of meaning? How did you handle that feeling?

4. What drives our craving for people's approval? How has that craving played out in your own life?

5. In your words, what's the connection between the human craving for significance and the human craving for happiness? How do you think these two longings are related?

Chapter 5: Our Enchanted Beginnings

1. What does the Bible tell us in Genesis 1:26–27? Why is this such an important passage?

2. God created humans to resemble and reflect him. What does that mean? How might that make you rethink the seemingly mundane moments of everyday life?

3. What does the Bible have to say about happiness? What is the role of happiness when it comes to faith in God?

4. If we really believed humans were immortal, how would that change the way we treat one another? What does it imply about the role of Christians in the cause of justice?

5. What is the "true place" that Pascal was referring to?

Chapter 6: Fallen to Where We Are

1. Chances are you've heard about sin before. What has been your common understanding of sin apart from what the Bible says about it? How do you think most people view sin?

2. When we put the several metaphors of sin together, the Bible portrays sin to be the "willful, personal snub of the God who made us." Why do you think that definition is hard for most people to accept?

3. What does it mean to suppress the knowledge of God?

4. In Deuteronomy 32, what does the Bible show us about ancient Israel's response to God's gracious provision? Have there been times in your life when you responded to God in similar ways?

5. What are the "two evils" mentioned in Jeremiah 2:13? Why do you think God calls these evil?

Chapter 7: Jesus

1. There is a lot of background to the New Testament; it's basically the entire Old Testament. What are some of the key events in the Old Testament that help us understand the identity of Jesus?

2. What are the different names and titles that are given to Jesus in the gospel of Matthew? What does each one teach us about the identity of Jesus?

3. In the gospel of John, Jesus is called "the Word" (1:1, 14). What does that mean? What does it tell us about Jesus's existence from eternity and his mission when he became a man?

4. The Bible teaches that Jesus is the perfect image of God (see Colossians 1:15). What do you think it means to perfectly image God? What does Jesus's perfect humanity mean for our own?

5. What does each of the following passages tell us about Jesus?

a. Matthew 1:16

b. Matthew 1:21

c. Matthew 1:22–23

d. Matthew 3:16–17

e. John 1:1–3, 14

f. Matthew 14:33

g. Colossians 1:15–20

h. Hebrews 1:1–3

i. John 14:9

Chapter 8: The Violent Rescue

1. Describe the showdown in 1 Kings 18 between Elijah and the 450 prophets of Baal. Imagine the hopelessness of the false prophets. What does this scene teach us about the condition of humans separated from God? Write a list of words that come to mind.

2. Why do you think there have been attempts within American Christianity to downplay the centrality of the crucifixion? What are some examples that you have seen?

3. Explain the difference between Jesus's active obedience and his passive obedience. What are some practical ways that both kinds of obedience should characterize our lives?

4. In the following passages, what does God show us about himself in the crucifixion of Jesus?

   a. Romans 3:24–26

   b. Romans 5:6–8

5. What does *penal substitution* mean? How does this describe what Jesus did in his death on the cross? Express in your own words what this means to you. What impact does it have on your life?

Chapter 9: He Didn't Stay Dead

1. What is a tragedy, and what purpose does it serve in literature? In what ways does the death of Jesus have all the makings of a tragic story? Why is it not a tragedy?

2. How does the resurrection of Jesus elevate the Christian story to be more than just a story?

3. What does it mean that our response to the gospel message is inherently personal?

4. The word *believe* is commonly used in contemporary English. What does it mean to believe according to the Bible? How should we think about faith in Jesus?

5. Imagine yourself stuck in a situation that feels impossible to solve. How does faith in Jesus help you in the midst of uncertainty and hardship?

Chapter 10: Hope Is Here

1. Paul wrote that by faith in Jesus, we "rejoice in hope of the glory of God" (Romans 5:2). According to the following passages, what assurance does God give us for this hope?
   a. Romans 5:5
   b. Romans 8:18–30
   c. Romans 15:13

2. The Holy Spirit, like Jesus, didn't just pop into existence when he stepped onto the stage of the New Testament. How should we think about the Spirit in view of his eternal existence in the Trinity?

3. Read John 14:15–27. How did Jesus encourage his disciples even when his death was imminent? Why do you think his words would have been an encouragement to them?

4. When someone believes in Jesus, that person is united to him.

What does it mean to be united to Jesus? What is the Spirit's role in this union?

5. What does it mean to rejoice not in circumstances but in hope? How does rejoicing in hope bring stability to the complexities of life in this world?

Chapter 11: Born All Over Again

1. What is the Holy Spirit's role when it comes to our faith in Jesus?
2. What is significant about receiving a new identity? How is something like an identity different from, say, mere behavior?
3. What difference does Jesus make in our pursuit of significance and happiness? If we were created to resemble and reflect the glory of God, how does Jesus restore that purpose in our lives?
4. Explain Augustine's happiness criteria. What role does the Holy Spirit fulfill in light of this criteria?
5. In your own words, how would you describe the meaning and joy found in knowing Jesus?

Acknowledgments

There are a few different settings that come to mind when I imagine the perfect place for writing acknowledgments. They're all quiet except for the melody of birds in the background. I'd be sitting back, reflective and smiling, enjoying the warmth of spring's glorious sun, and in that restful moment, with all that tranquility, the gratitude would flow like a torrent. And they'd be great acknowledgments.

But I'm not there right now, not even close.

I've found a way to throw these paragraphs down only because of the principle that gratitude, if it's real, doesn't need the perfect place for its expression. I've thought before that if what I've got to say doesn't work in the hardest times, then it's probably not worth saying. When it comes to gratitude, if we're waiting for that ideal setting before we can speak up, there are going to be a lot of underappreciated people in our wake.

So because I'm thankful—really, simply thankful—allow me to try my best to say what I can remember right now about all the people who have made this book possible.

Most importantly, Jesus is the One at work here. He's behind all this, and he's more alive in this exact moment than you or me or anyone. He knows we only scratch the surface of his realness. All my other thank-yous are just me talking about gifts he's given me.

Thank you to my wife, Melissa, for your love, for your honesty, and for all the little things you do that help me think straight. My life is so blessed because of you, for so many reasons.

And to our children, Elizabeth, Hannah, Micah, John Owen, Noah,

Ava, and Nathaniel—I never knew I could be this rich. Being your dad is one of my greatest honors.

To my mom and dad, Phil and Jana, and to my in-laws, Ms. Pam and Mr. David, thank you for your abiding love and unremitting support, even as Melissa and I have moved a swarm of your grandchildren so many miles away. We love and appreciate you so much.

Thank you to my fellow pastors at Cities Church in Minneapolis. I love and admire you. Thanks in particular to David Mathis, who was my editor and boss at desiringGod.org when the seed for this book fell to the ground. Thanks also to Joe Rigney for his helpful advice on an earlier section of writing and to Tony Reinke, who took the time to lead me through a writer's block, one not of emptiness but of clutter. Thanks to Marshall Segal and Jon Bloom, and to the whole team at desiringGod.org, who care so much about saying true and wonderful things about God. Thank you, John Piper, for your influence and continued encouragement, both in writing and pastoral ministry. And thank you, Tony Anderson, for your music that snapped me back to reality more than a few times.

Thank you to Bruce Nygren and the amazing team at Multnomah for this opportunity. Thank you, Bruce, for your gracious nudging early on that has made this book better. It has been such a privilege to work with you.

Thanks also to my team of readers who subscribed to receive updates about this project a good while ago. Your interest and feedback at every turn have been like gusts of wind in my sails. You answered my questions and prayed for me, and I am so grateful.

Finally, thanks to David Cooper, to whom this book is dedicated. Thank you, brother, for being such a faithful friend and for investing in my life so many years ago. Not only did you disciple me, but you also showed me what it means to be a servant like Jesus for others. You showed me what it means to rejoice not that the spirits are subject to us but that our names are written in heaven (see Luke 10:20). Every morning when I pray Psalm 51, that God will restore to me the joy of his salvation, I think of you and ask, *Father in heaven, make me glad in you, like David Cooper is. Amen.*

Notes

Chapter 1: The Stupid Normal

1. *Calculated barrenness* is the term Doug Wilson has given to our culture's alternative platform to God's fruitfulness mandate in Genesis 1:28. Douglas Wilson, *Father Hunger: Why God Calls Men to Love and Lead Their Families* (Nashville: Thomas Nelson, 2012), 155.
2. Charles Taylor, *A Secular Age* (Cambridge, MA: Belknap Press of Harvard University Press, 2007), 542.
3. Walt Whitman, "Song of Myself," *Leaves of Grass,* 1855, http://whitmanarchive.org/published/LG/figures/ppp.00271.021.jpg.
4. Timothy Keller, *Making Sense of God: An Invitation to the Skeptical* (New York: Penguin, 2016), 3.
5. The Strumbellas, "Spirits," copyright © 2015, Glassnote.
6. Taylor, *Secular Age,* 19–20. Taylor explained that although self-sufficing humanisms existed in the past, our current secular age is unique with its brazen "exclusive humanism." He wrote, "I'm talking about an age [this secular age] when self-sufficing humanism becomes a widely available option, which it never was in the ancient world, where only a small minority of the élite which was itself a minority espoused it. . . . A secular age is one in which the eclipse of all goals beyond human flourishing becomes conceivable; or better, it falls within the range of the imaginable life for masses of people." Taylor, *Secular Age,* 19–20. See also 233–34.
7. G. K. Chesterton, *Orthodoxy* (Louisville, KY: GLH Publishing, 2016), 64.
8. Blaise Pascal, *Pensées and Other Writings,* ed. Anthony Levi, trans. Honor Levi (New York: Oxford University Press, 1995), 51.
9. Augustine, sermon 306, quoted in Thomas A. Hand, *Augustine on Prayer* (New York: Catholic Book Publishing, 1986), 13.
10. Jonathan Haidt, *The Happiness Hypothesis: Finding Modern Truth in Ancient Wisdom* (New York: Basic Books, 2006), x.
11. Haidt, *Happiness Hypothesis,* 216–17.
12. Haidt, *Happiness Hypothesis,* 238 (emphasis added).
13. Dorothy Sayers, "The Greatest Drama Ever Staged Is the Official Creed of Christendom," Catholic Education Resource Center, originally

published in the *Sunday Times,* April 2, 1938, www.catholiceducation
.org/en/religion-and-philosophy/apologetics/the-greatest-drama-ever
-stages-is-the-official-creed-of-christendom.html.

14. Kevin J. Vanhoozer, *Faith Speaking Understanding: Performing the
Drama of Doctrine* (Louisville, KY: Westminster John Knox, 2014), 29.

Chapter 2: When You Think About God

1. Daniel Kahneman, *Thinking, Fast and Slow* (New York: Farrar, Straus,
and Giroux, 2011), 51.

2. A. W. Tozer, *The Knowledge of the Holy* (New York: HarperOne, 2009), 1.

Chapter 3: The Happy Father Who Loves

1. Michael Reeves, *Delighting in the Trinity: An Introduction to the
Christian Faith* (Downers Grove, IL: IVP Academic, 2012), 21.

2. Christian Reformed Church, *Ecumenical Creeds and Reformed Confes-
sions* (Grand Rapids, MI: Faith Alive Christian Resources, 1987), 9.

3. Matthew Levering, *The Theology of Augustine: An Introductory Guide to
His Most Important Works* (Minneapolis: Baker Academic, 2013), 7. In
his essay on the Trinity, Jonathan Edwards wrote, "Christ is called the
face of God (Exod. 33:14): the word in the original signifies face, looks,
form or appearance. Now what can be so properly and fitly called so with
respect to God as God's own perfect idea of Himself whereby He has
every moment a view of His own essence: this idea is that 'face of God'
which God sees as a man sees his own face in a looking glass. 'Tis of such
form or appearance whereby God eternally appears to Himself." Edwards,
"An Unpublished Essay on the Trinity," Christian Classics Ethereal
Library, www.ccel.org/ccel/edwards/trinity/files/trinity.html.

4. Levering, *Theology of Augustine,* 62.

Chapter 4: Starting with a Search

1. Anthony Levi, introduction to *Pensées and Other Writings,* by Blaise
Pascal, ed. Anthony Levi, trans. Honor Levi (New York: Oxford University Press, 1995), vii.

2. Pascal, *Pensées and Other Writings,* 8.

3. John Piper, *Don't Waste Your Life* (Wheaton, IL: Crossway, 2007), 47.

4. Charles Taylor, *A Secular Age* (Cambridge, MA: Belknap Press of
Harvard University Press, 2007), 299.

5. Paul Michael Barry and James Bay, "Let It Go," copyright © 2015, Universal Music Publishing Group.
6. Timothy B. Savage, *Power Through Weakness: Paul's Understanding of the Christian Ministry in 2 Corinthians* (Cambridge, UK: Cambridge University Press, 2004), 22–23.
7. Savage, *Power Through Weakness,* 65.
8. Pascal, *Pensées and Other Writings,* 51.
9. Travis Jerome Goff and Travis Meadows, "What We Ain't Got," copyright © 2013, Songs of Universal Inc./Red Vinyl Music.
10. Pascal, *Pensées and Other Writings,* 8.

Chapter 5: Our Enchanted Beginnings
1. G. K. Beale, *A New Testament Biblical Theology: The Unfolding of the Old Testament in the New* (Grand Rapids, MI: Baker, 2011), 31.
2. Clive Aslet, "Our Picture of Her Majesty Will Never Fade," *Telegraph,* May 21, 2014, www.telegraph.co.uk/news/uknews/queen-elizabeth-II/10844075/Our-picture-of-Her-Majesty-will-never-fade.html.
3. John Piper has listed several examples where the affections are woven into divine commands, such as to do "acts of mercy, *with cheerfulness*" (Romans 12:8) or to be a "*cheerful* giver" (2 Corinthians 9:7). Other texts include Deuteronomy 28:47; 1 Chronicles 16:31, 33; Nehemiah 8:10; Psalm 32:11; 33:1; 35:9; 40:8, 16; 42:1–2; 63:1, 11; 64:10; 95:1; 97:1, 12; 98:4; 104:34; 105:3; Isaiah 41:16; Joel 2:23; Micah 6:8; Zechariah 2:10; 10:7; Acts 20:35; 2 Corinthians 2:3; Philippians 3:1; 4:4; Hebrews 10:34; 13:17; 1 Peter 5:2. John Piper, *Desiring God: Meditations of a Christian Hedonist* (Sisters, OR: Multnomah, 2003), 25 (italics in original).
4. C. S. Lewis, *Reflections on the Psalms* (New York: HarperOne, 2017), 112.
5. C. S. Lewis, *God in the Dock* (Grand Rapids, MI: Eerdmans, 2014), 28.
6. C. S. Lewis, *The Weight of Glory* (New York: HarperOne, 2015), 47.

Chapter 6: Fallen to Where We Are
1. D. A. Carson, "Sin's Contemporary Significance," in *Fallen: A Theology of Sin,* ed. Christopher W. Morgan and Robert A. Peterson (Wheaton, IL: Crossway, 2013), 29.
2. Gary A. Anderson, *Sin: A History* (New Haven, CT: Yale University Press, 2009), 16.

3. John W. Mahony, "A Theology of Sin for Today," in *Fallen,* 195. My section on the two categories of sin is indebted to John Mahony's treatment of this topic.

4. Cornelius Plantinga Jr., *Not the Way It's Supposed to Be: A Breviary of Sin* (Grand Rapids, MI: Eerdmans, 1996), 13.

5. John Webster, *Holiness* (Grand Rapids, MI: Eerdmans, 2003), 84.

6. "We don't believe instead of doubting; we believe while doubting. We're all Thomas now. . . . Most of us live in this cross-pressured space, where both our agnosticism and our devotion are mutually haunted and haunting." James K. A. Smith, *How (Not) to Be Secular: Reading Charles Taylor* (Grand Rapids, MI: Eerdmans, 2014), 4.

7. David Foster Wallace, "All That," *New Yorker,* December 14, 2009, www.newyorker.com/magazine/2009/12/14/all-that-2.

8. Matt Jenson, *The Gravity of Sin: Augustine, Luther and Barth on* Homo Incurvatus in Se (London: T & T Clark, 2006).

9. Bruce Marshall, *The World, the Flesh, and Father Smith* (Boston: Houghton Mifflin, 1945), 108.

Chapter 7: Jesus

1. H. A. Ironside, *Expository Notes on the Gospel of Matthew* (Neptune, NJ: Loizeaux Brothers, 1948), 14. The Hebrew name *Yeshua* is our English name Joshua, which is the equivalent of the Spanish name Jesús.

2. Frederick Buechner, *Secrets in the Dark: A Life in Sermons* (New York: HarperCollins, 2007), 28.

3. "The coming King would do two main things, according to a variety of texts and as we study a variety of actual would-be royal movements within history. First, he would build or restore the Temple. Second, he would fight the decisive battle against the enemy." N. T. Wright, *The Challenge of Jesus: Rediscovering Who Jesus Was and Is* (Downers Grove, IL: InterVarsity, 1999), 76.

4. Richard B. Hays, *Reading Backwards: Figural Christology and the Fourfold Gospel Witness* (Waco, TX: Baylor University Press, 2014), 44.

5. Richard Bauckham, *God Crucified: Monotheism and Christology in the New Testament* (Grand Rapids, MI: Eerdmans, 1999), 6.

6. "The magi (2:2, 11), a leper seeking healing (8:2), a ruler of the synagogue (9:18), the Canaanite woman (15:25), the mother of James and John (20:20), the two Marys who first encounter the Risen Lord (28:9),

and the disciples at the resurrection appearance on a mountain in Galilee (28:17)." Hays, *Reading Backwards,* 44.

7. Hays, *Reading Backwards,* 47.

8. "Jesus Christ confronts us in the *whole fact,* as true God and true man. The Word of God comes to us in Jesus Christ, and so personally and with such authority and majesty, that we are given to know Jesus Christ as God himself, and here we know that we know God only by God." T. F. Torrance, *Incarnation: The Person and Life of Christ* (Downers Grove, IL: InterVarsity, 2008), 36 (emphasis in the original).

9. "Jesus' deity did not spring forth from the resolution of any church council, but rests in eternity past. So he never *became* God; he was always God, and he *became* human, the man Jesus of Nazareth." Michael F. Bird et al., *How God Became Jesus: The Real Origins of Belief in Jesus' Divine Nature—A Response to Bart D. Ehrman* (Grand Rapids, MI: Zondervan, 2014), 12 (emphasis in the original).

Chapter 8: The Violent Rescue

1. Fleming Rutledge, *The Crucifixion: Understanding the Death of Jesus Christ* (Grand Rapids, MI: Eerdmans, 2015), 3.

2. Rutledge, *Crucifixion,* 31.

3. See Jonathan Parnell, "Anger," in *Killjoys: The Seven Deadly Sins,* ed. Marshall Segal (Minneapolis: Desiring God, 2014), 35–47.

4. God's love for his glory and his love for us are deeply intertwined. For God to be most committed to his glory means that he is most committed to the very thing that makes us happy. In other words, his commitment to his glory is his commitment to the everlasting happiness of his people, which is loving. For more on this topic, check out my article "Call That Love," desiringGod.org, May 25, 2015, www.desiringgod.org/articles/call -that-love.

5. D. A. Carson, interview by David Mathis, "The Doctrine of the Wrath of God," podcast video, desiringGod.org, January 5, 2012, www.desiring god.org/interviews/the-doctrine-of-the-wrath-of-god.

6. "Knowing or seeing the Father is centrally knowing God's redeeming act in Christ. It is the soteriological function of Christ that is the focus of the New Testament. Jesus reveals God as the God who saves his people. Revelation and redemption go hand in hand across the canon." Richard Lints, *Identity and Idolatry: The Image of God and Its Inversion* (Downers Grove, IL: InterVarsity, 2015), 120.

7. For more on how Jesus's death defeated Satan and how that relates to the meaning of propitiation, see Sinclair B. Ferguson, "Christus Victor et Propitiator: The Death of Christ, Substitute and Conqueror," in *For the Fame of God's Name: Essays in Honor of John Piper,* ed. Sam Storms and Justin Taylor (Wheaton, IL: Crossway, 2010), 171–189. I agree with D. A. Carson that propitiation "holds together all the other biblical ways of talking about the cross." D. A. Carson, *Scandalous: The Cross and Resurrection of Jesus* (Wheaton, IL: Crossway, 2010), 67.

8. In Romans 3:25, some English translations replace "propitiation" with "sacrifice of atonement" (NIV, NRSV). Both translations have the right idea. We know Paul was talking about atonement and saying that Jesus was a sacrifice for sinners like us. The different translations have to do with the certainty surrounding *the kind of sacrifice* Jesus was. There were two kinds in the Old Testament. First was *propitiation,* which is directed at God, and second was *expiation,* which is directed at people. Propitiation has to do with satisfying the righteous anger of God. It's the part that pays the debt, that makes reparations. It means that God's anger toward sinners like us is gone. It's no more. Expiation has to do with the removal of sin. It means that the muck of our sin, the sin that defames God's glory and debases ourselves, is gone. It's no more. Overall, the Bible teaches that Jesus did both when he died in our place. He took God's wrath upon himself, and he removed our sins from us. But I think propitiation is specifically what Paul had in view in Romans 3.

9. D. A. Carson, *Scandalous: The Cross and Resurrection of Jesus* (Wheaton, IL: Crossway, 2010), 60.

10. Leon Morris explained that propitiation was given a new meaning in the Bible because the biblical authors knew God was different from pagan deities. "To the men of the Old Testament the wrath of God is both very real and very serious. God is not thought of as capriciously angry (like the deities of the heathen), but, because He is a moral Being." Leon Morris, *The Apostolic Preaching of the Cross* (Grand Rapids, MI: Eerdmans, 1965), 149.

11. "The biblical gospel of atonement is of God satisfying himself by substituting himself for us." John R. W. Stott, *The Cross of Christ* (Downers Grove, IL: InterVarsity, 2006), 159.

Chapter 9: He Didn't Stay Dead

1. Herman Melville, *Billy Budd, Sailor and Selected Tales* (Oxford: Oxford University Press, 1962), 288. There is an element of hope in Melville's

story I should mention, even a sort of "resurrection," critics argue. Melville wrote, "At the same moment [when Billy was executed] it chanced that the vapory fleece hanging low in the East was shot through with a soft glory as of the fleece of the Lamb of God seen in mystical vision, and simultaneously therewith, watched by the wedged mass of upturned faces, Billy ascended; and, ascending, took the full rose of the dawn." Melville, *Billy Budd, Sailor,* 354.

2. The Resurrection is the foundation of the entire book of Acts and the consistent message of the apostles (see Acts 1:22; 2:32). In fact, one criterion for being an apostle was witnessing the Resurrection (see 1:22). The Resurrection is also the event that validates the identity of Jesus (see Romans 1:4). He is "both Lord and Christ" because he was raised from the dead (Acts 2:36). David Peterson wrote, "The ultimate indication of his true identity are his resurrection and ascension to God's right hand, understood from a scriptural perspective." David G. Peterson, *The Acts of the Apostles* (Grand Rapids, MI: Eerdmans, 2009), 58–59. I think the resurrection of Jesus had a particular impact on Peter based on how he was portrayed at the end of Luke and beginning of Acts. For more on that, check out my sermon "Not the Same," Cities Church, Minneapolis, MN, February 1, 2015, www.citieschurch.com/sermons/2015/2/11/not -the-same.

3. See John Milbank, "The Ethics of Self-Sacrifice," *First Things,* March 1999, www.firstthings.com/article/1999/03/004-the-ethics-of-self -sacrifice. Milbank explained that the hope of resurrection is essential for meaningful self-sacrifice.

4. Kevin J. Vanhoozer, *The Drama of Doctrine: A Canonical Linguistic Approach to Christian Doctrine* (Louisville, KY: Westminster John Knox, 2005), 115.

5. We see this especially in the book of Acts. Just because Jesus was raised and therefore not rubbing shoulders with the apostles, we should not think he was somehow not part of the gospel's advance. Jesus is still very much at work in the lives of his people, both from heaven where he reigns and through his Spirit on earth. Speaking of Jesus's ascension to heaven, Alan Thompson wrote, "The focus here is not on [Jesus's] 'absence' and consequent 'inactivity,' but rather on the 'place' from which Jesus rules for the rest of Acts." Alan Thompson, *The Acts of the Risen Lord Jesus: Luke's Account of God's Unfolding Plan* (Downers Grove, IL: IVP Academic, 2011), 49. Tim Chester and Jonny Woodrow explained, "Christ ascends

into heaven at the beginning of the book of Acts, but he is not then absent from the story. On a number of occasions he intervenes from heaven and these prove to be key moments in the story." Tim Chester and Jonny Woodrow, *The Ascension: Humanity in the Presence of God* (Ross-shire, Scotland: Christian Focus Publications, 2013), 49.

Over and over again in the book of Acts, we see that Jesus was taking a prominent role in how the events unfolded. It was Jesus himself who confronted Saul on his way to Damascus in chapter 9. In amazing irony, Jesus turned his most ardent human opponent into his most zealous missionary. In another instance of conversion, Jesus was said to be the One who opened Lydia's heart (see 16:14). And then later, when Paul was in Jerusalem and found himself discouraged in the barracks, "the Lord stood by him and said, 'Take courage, for as you have testified to the facts about me in Jerusalem, so you must testify also in Rome'" (23:11). Jesus was the One who spoke comfort to Paul.

So whether in conversion (opening hearts) or in sustaining the mission (encouraging us), Jesus is at work in his church.
6. This illustration is adapted from Lesslie Newbigin, *Proper Confidence: Faith, Doubt and Certainty in Christian Discipleship* (Grand Rapids, MI: Eerdmans, 1995), 11.
7. Jonathan Edwards, *A Treatise Concerning the Religious Affections* (Philadelphia: James Crissy, 1821), 245.
8. "If the ground of saving faith is 'the light of the gospel of the glory of Christ,' and if the concept of 'glory' involves Christ's moral *beauty* and excellency, then saving faith must flow from a sense or perception of beauty, not merely a validation of facts." John Piper, "Is Faith a Way of Seeing?," desiringGod.org, April 1, 1977, www.desiringgod.org/articles/is-faith-a-way-of-seeing (emphasis in the original).
9. John Piper, *Future Grace: The Purifying Power of the Promises of God,* rev. ed. (Colorado Springs, CO: Multnomah, 2012), 209. In contrast, *believe* is used only "eleven times in Matthew, twelve in Mark, and nine in Luke." Piper, *Future Grace,* 209.

Chapter 10: Hope Is Here
1. John Piper, *Future Grace: The Purifying Power of the Promises of God,* rev. ed. (Colorado Springs, CO: Multnomah, 2012), 6.
2. Paul called the Spirit our "guarantee" in Ephesians 1:13–14: "In him you also, when you heard the word of truth, the gospel of your salvation, and

believed in him, were sealed with the promised Holy Spirit, who is the guarantee of our inheritance until we acquire possession of it, to the praise of his glory." See also 2 Corinthians 1:22.

3. Different Christian traditions have swung all over the spectrum when it comes to understanding who the Spirit is and what he's doing here. In recent years, several books have been written at the popular level to recover a correct view of him, attempting to gain ground lost by Christians who have marginalized him or just flat out seen him sideways. Most recently, see Francis Chan, *Forgotten God: Reversing Our Tragic Neglect of the Holy Spirit* (Colorado Springs, CO: David C Cook, 2009) and J. D. Greear, *Jesus, Continued . . . : Why the Spirit Inside You Is Better Than Jesus Beside You* (Grand Rapids, MI: Zondervan, 2014).

4. Sinclair Ferguson summarizes the Holy Spirit's activity in the Old Testament: "The Spirit of God is the executive of the powerful presence of God in the governing of the created order." Sinclair B. Ferguson, *The Holy Spirit: Contours of Christian Theology* (Downers Grove, IL: InterVarsity, 1996), 21.

5. Jonathan Edwards, "An Unpublished Essay on the Trinity," Christian Classics Ethereal Library, www.ccel.org/ccel/edwards/trinity/files/trinity.html.

6. Ferguson, *Holy Spirit*, 16.

7. Both Augustine and Edwards mined deeply to understand the Trinity. As I was writing this chapter, I wondered if Edwards (1703–1758) ever read Augustine (354–430) as a source. So I texted my friend and fellow pastor Joe Rigney for some help. This is how he responded:

> William Ames and Cotton Mather were probably the nearest sources for Edwards. I'm not sure if he ever read Augustine directly. He does use the psychological image [of the Trinity] in some different ways from Augustine. To put it simply, Augustine predicated attributes of the single divine essence (i.e., wisdom is an essence/substance term), and then appropriated specific terms to persons (usually based on the economy of redemption). Thus the Son is the wisdom of God by appropriation, but the Father is also wisdom by divine simplicity. The Son is wisdom from wisdom.
>
> Edwards on the other hand reduces attributes to persons. Thus, the Son *is* the wisdom of God, and the Father only has wisdom by virtue of being "in" the Son *(perichoresis)*. Augustine

explicitly rejects that sort of move. I think they wind up in the same place, but they do so with different challenges/mysteries. . . . Augustine is simply going to be more careful about pressing on some of these issues, and more apt to lean on the economy of redemption. Edwards, while allowing for lots of mystery, presses harder." Joe Rigney, text message to author, December 22, 2015.

8. The doctrine of Jesus's ascension has long been a staple in the orthodox understanding of Jesus's life and work. The Bible clearly tells us that Jesus is seated at the right hand of the Father in the heavenly places (see Luke 22:69; Acts 2:33; 5:31; Romans 8:34; Ephesians 1:20; Colossians 3:1; Hebrews 1:3). In fact, we could even say that Jesus's ascension is an indispensable part of the gospel.

Tim Chester and Jonny Woodrow give three crucial truths about Jesus's ascension: He is the ascended priest, completing a perfect sacrifice. He is our ascended king, reigning over all. And he is the ascended man, fulfilling the glory of humanity for which we were created. The ascension matters for our salvation because if Jesus's sacrifice is to be effective, his kingship is to be real, and his humanity is to be glorified, *he must be ascended.* See Tim Chester and Jonny Woodrow, *The Ascension: Humanity in the Presence of God* (Ross-shire, Scotland: Christian Focus Publications, 2013).

9. Just a few verses before Jesus talked about the Spirit, we read Jesus's dialogue with Philip: "Philip said to him, 'Lord, show us the Father, and it is enough for us.' Jesus said to him, 'Have I been with you so long, and you still do not know me, Philip? Whoever has seen me has seen the Father. How can you say, "Show us the Father"?'" (John 14:8–9).

10. We see the same connection between God's love and the Holy Spirit in 1 John 4:12–13: "No one has ever seen God; if we love one another, God abides in us and his love is perfected in us. By this we know that we abide in him and he in us, because he has given us of his Spirit." Edwards commented, "'Tis the same argument in both verses. In the 12th verse the apostle argues that if we have love dwelling in us we have God dwelling in us, and in the 13th verse He clears the force of the argument by this that love is God's Spirit." Edwards, "An Unpublished Essay on the Trinity."

Chapter 11: Born All Over Again

1. Paul used this expression and its variations about 160 times. See Sinclair B. Ferguson, *The Holy Spirit: Contours of Christian Theology* (Downers Grove, IL: InterVarsity, 1996), 100.

2. See Ezekiel 36:25–27; John 1:12–13; 3:3–8; 2 Corinthians 5:17; Titus 3:5; James 1:18; 1 Peter 1:3, 22–25; 1 John 2:29; 3:9; 4:7; 5:1–4, 18.

3. Peter wrote in 2 Peter 1:3–4, "[God's] divine power has granted to us all things that pertain to life and godliness, through the knowledge of him who called us to his own glory and excellence, by which he has granted to us his precious and very great promises, *so that through them you may become partakers of the divine nature,* having escaped from the corruption that is in the world because of sinful desire." He also said of himself in 1 Peter 5:1, "So I exhort the elders among you, as a fellow elder and a witness of the sufferings of Christ, *as well as a partaker in the glory that is going to be revealed."*

4. Thomas A. Hand, *Augustine on Prayer* (New York: Catholic Book Publishing, 1986), 16.

5. Hand, *Augustine on Prayer,* 5 (emphasis added).

6. "Gratitude exclaims, very properly, 'How good of God to give me this.' Adoration says, 'What must be the quality of that Being whose far-off and momentary coruscations are like this!' One's mind runs back up the sunbeam to the sun.'" C. S. Lewis, *Letters to Malcolm: Chiefly on Prayer* (Boston: Houghton Mifflin Harcourt, 2002), 90.

Epilogue: The Path Together

1. David Mathis, *Habits of Grace: Enjoying Jesus Through the Spiritual Disciplines* (Wheaton, IL: Crossway, 2016).

2. Joe Rigney, *The Things of Earth: Treasuring God by Enjoying His Gifts* (Wheaton, IL: Crossway, 2014).

Study Guide

1. Alexis de Tocqueville, *Democracy in America,* trans. Phillips Bradley (New York: Vintage, 1990), 2:139.

Topical Index

Scripture Index